Designing New Traditions In Quilts

by Sharyn Squier Craig

CHITRA PUBLICATIONS

Chitra Publications
301 Church Street
New Milford, Pennsylvania 18834

First printing: 1991

Library of Congress Cataloging-in-Publication Data.

Craig, Sharyn Squier, 1947-
    Designing new traditions in quilts / by Sharyn Squier Craig
        p.   cm.
    Includes bibliographical references.
    ISBN 0-9622565-1-X : $24.95
    1. Quilting. 2. Patchwork. I. Title.
TT835.C73   1991
746.9'7--dc20

                                                            91-14621
                                                              CIP

Editors: Jack Braunstein and Jane Townswick
Designer: Rebecca Miller-Baum
Illustrator: Pamela Moss Watts

*Cover Quilt: "Creativity In Motion" by Sharyn Squier Craig.
Photographed by Ken Jacques.*

❖ Without the constant love and support of my husband George and my children, Amy and Tom, this book would never have become a reality. They believed in me even when I doubted myself. Special thanks, also, to Tom and Marie Craig for raising a son who feels so secure in his own abilities that he is capable of accepting and encouraging me in mine. I give thanks, too, to my own parents, Frank and Pauline Squier, for their unconditional love, support and encouragement—and for teaching me that I could do anything and everything I set my mind to.

The soul of quilting lies in the bonds that it offers to people from all walks of life, of all races and generations. Quilts link us with our grandmothers, as well as our children and grandchildren yet to come. I would like to dedicate this book to all quilting students and enthusiasts, especially all of the students I have taught over the years. It is because of you and for you that I have constantly kept striving to learn more and become a better teacher. I offer to each of you the challenge to reach out a little higher with each new quilt. I thank you, too, for letting me tap into your creative energies, and for allowing me to share some of your quilts in this book.

To quilters everywhere—may all your days be filled with visions of quilts and the time to work on them!

Foreword

The Secret of Sharyn Craig's Creativity...

❖ Quiltmaking is an art, the expression of beauty according to aesthetic principles, and a craft, an art requiring special skill. Beginning quilters are often preoccupied with such definitions, and this can hinder growth. Why not simply appreciate elements in every quilt we see? Thus, we expand our own creativity.

Sharyn Craig taught herself to work this way from the beginning. By borrowing combinations of colors or shapes from antique quilts she'd seen in books and magazines, Sharyn discovered what she likes in her own quilts. She also discovered how to stretch one idea into another quilt pattern. Sharyn sees possibilities everywhere, and so do the thousands of students she has taught. She is one of the few quilt teachers I've met who successfully teaches students to be creative. Students come out of her classes with finished, one-of-a-kind quilt tops. They are excited and finish these quilts almost immediately, then they sign up for more of Sharyn's classes. They become creative quiltmakers who make many, many quilts.

Sharyn has learned what past quiltmakers knew. In passing around their patterns and sharing their quilts among family members, each quiltmaker inspired another. They kept what they liked and added a touch of individual taste to the patterns, thus creating original designs. These are the antique quilts we most admire today, those that are a bit askew or draw the eye to one corner, even quilts made in outrageous colors that, surprisingly, work. These are the quilts that inspire Sharyn Craig.

You can make original quilts, too. We all have natural abilities which can flourish with practice. Creativity can be learned, and you do not have to start at square one. Sharyn Craig has proven that over and over again.

Patti Bachelder, Editor
Quilting Today, Traditional Quiltworks,
and *Miniature Quilts* magazines

Contents

Introduction vi

Getting Started 10

What If...? Doors To Creativity 14

Quilts and Their Inspirations 18

Single Irish Chain 19

Rails & Fences 22

Bow Ties 24

Double Irish Chain 27

Ohio Star 28

Bear's Paw 30

Pine Tree 33

Terrific Triangles 34

One Patch 37

Ocean Waves 38

LeMoyne Star 40

Sawtooth Baskets 42

Feathered Stars 43

Pineapple 44

Medallion 45

Sisterhood 46

Confetti 49

Attic Windows 50

Pyramids Plus 52

Hawaiian Flag 57

Now It's Your Turn 60

What If...? Design Challenges 64

Credits 93

Suggested Reading 94

Introduction

❖ My goal in writing this book is to encourage you to become a more creative quilter. It's easier than you think! "Creativity is the ability to cause something to come into being." We *all* possess this ability; it is not rationed out to just certain people. We are always making creative decisions in our lives, from deciding what type of clothing to wear, to major decisions about decorating an entire home.

To make our own creative choices in quiltmaking, we simply need a bit of information and the desire to make a quilt that is unlike anyone else's. Once we get our creative juices started, they will keep on flowing!

It's easy to become a "recipe quilter," following patterns and directions that tell us exactly how much fabric is needed, the size of the quilt, what borders and settings to use, etc. Following patterns and directions is a great way to learn, but these are *someone else's* creative choices. I want to show you that *you* can learn to make these types of creative decisions on your own!

For me, quiltmaking is like Christmas morning—always full of anticipation, surprises and lots of fun! I love surprises—and a quilt that develops as it grows is sure to be filled with many of them! (Some surprises are better than others, but they are all exciting and fun!)

Doing something a bit differently means taking risks—risking some fabric, possibly, or the security of using a "proven" pattern. The first time you start making a quilt without having any idea of where it's going, you might be a bit scared—but you don't need all the answers before you start. As long as you have the desire to begin your quilting adventure, you'll be prepared to go wherever it takes you!

Being creative means taking risks but it also means taking control. A quilt should be *your* personal statement, reflecting *your* color choices, block preferences, border design, etc. As I once heard Christal Carter say, "A creative person is one who is willing to be a little weird." It doesn't matter whether you're making traditional or abstract statements, as long as they're *your* statements.

One of my friends in high school was an extremely creative person who expressed her creativity by wearing clothing she had designed herself. She liked to combine pieces from many different patterns, resulting in a totally unique look. Everyone admired her ability to make something special. Years later, I discovered that she had become an attorney and then a judge. As I told her of my life in quiltmaking, she looked at me wistfully and declared that she had lost all her creativity. I was stunned! At first, I didn't believe her—after all, how can creativity just "go away"? Then I realized what she meant. She hadn't really *lost* her creativity—she had just allowed it to become dormant through lack of exercise. She could become creative once more, simply by *using* her innate creative abilities.

I have experienced similar feelings about my creative ability in the kitchen. As a newlywed, I loved to cook and experiment with new foods, but my husband would never taste anything he could not identify. Eventually, I developed a "Why bother?" attitude and, as a result, the thought of being creative in the kitchen now seems overwhelming to me.

Yet, what if I *did* want to become more creative in the arts of cooking and dining? I would head for the bookstore and the library to find books with delectable recipes and pictures of elegantly set tables. I'd ask friends for their favorite recipes and investigate adult education classes—in short, *I would look for inspiration*.

For inspiration in quiltmaking, we can also turn to books and classes, as well as magazines, shows and guilds. Visual stimulation is vital nourishment for imagination and creativity. In this book, I hope to show you how to use visual stimulation as a catalyst that, along with a few simple tools, will enable you to branch out on your own as a quiltmaker and begin your own "new traditions" in quiltmaking!

Getting Started

Getting Started

❖ How do you begin making an original quilt, one that is different from everyone else's? I like to start with a well-organized workspace. I find it difficult to turn creativity on and off like a light switch, and a well-organized workspace allows me the freedom to think about the project at hand. I have my tools and materials carefully organized on shelves and in files. I like my table space to be clear as well, and ready for the new project. Tidying up my sewing area and beginning a new quilt are always beneficial for me—I update my files, straighten out my fabric collection, and make sure that everything is "just so." That way, there are no unfinished projects in sight to distract me, and I am able to focus entirely on new ideas.

I am lucky enough to have an entire room for my sewing area, but you don't need a whole room for your sewing area to be organized. A few sturdy shirt boxes will serve you very well. They can be used to store blocks as they are completed, and you can keep fabrics associated with particular quilts in them. Labeling each box according to the pattern or the name of the quilt can be a timesaver as well.

The goal is to work in an atmosphere that is conducive to fresh, new ideas. Decide what makes your sewing area work for you and take the time to set things up the way you like them, before you begin a new quilt. That way, your new project can be started with enthusiasm!

Looking for Inspiration

Once my working environment is ready, I turn to sources of visual stimulation to get my creative wheels turning. For me, pictures of antique quilts are a never-ending source of inspiration—for everything from block patterns to sets and color combinations. I have found that I'm as addicted to buying books as I am to buying fabric and making quilts! I look at pictures again and again, each time discovering something new and unique. My favorite source of photos is the annual Quilt

Engagement Calendar (published by E.P. Dutton). I can never bring myself to use these wonderful "picture books" as calendars! They are constant sources of visual stimulation.

Magazines are great resources, too. For years I have subscribed to magazines such as *Quilting Today, Traditional Quiltworks, Lady's Circle Patchwork Quilts* and *Country Living*. I saved so many issues that my husband eventually started making subtle comments about the world's paper shortage! When he finally threatened to have the fire department condemn our home as a fire hazard, I got the message and decided to thin out the collection.

I swallowed hard and dove through issue after issue, tearing out only those pictures I *really* wanted. The four-foot stack of magazines dwindled to a one-inch pile of loose pictures, and the results were exhilarating! Not only did the collection of quilt pictures become immediately more accessible, but the additional space I gained on the shelves could be used for storing more fabric! I highly recommend doing the same with your magazine collection. Keep the true quilt publications (even with torn-out pages) for reference, and discard all magazines that are not quilt-specific.

I inserted all the pictures I wanted to save into page protectors and stored them in looseleaf notebooks, organized according to pattern type: Feathered Stars, Log Cabins, etc. I put other pages into general notebooks, especially those with several interesting, unrelated quilts in one photo. Studying pictures of quilts can always bring inspiration, even for projects you are already working on. Today I hardly think twice about tearing pictures out of current magazines, and my collection of photos and patterns continues to grow.

Visual stimulation need not be just in the form of quilts. Nature is an infinite source of inspiration—a stroll through a garden can be an overwhelming sensory experience. Close observation of the subtle gradations of color in the petals of a single flower can be mind-boggling! Glancing through vacation pictures will bring back memories and inspire visual images and new ideas. I also love to glance through my art books and notice how painters use color and texture. I wish I could find a fabric as beautiful as Monet's "Waterlilies." Whether it's a picture of a vase of flowers or a quilt—if it works for you, use it to start your creative juices flowing!

Listening to Inspiration

When I want to start a new quilt, I leaf slowly through the pages of my notebooks, freeing my mind of any preconceived notions about what I want to find. I listen for photographs of quilts to speak to me in a nonspecific, emotional sense, in much the same way that some fabrics call out, "Buy me, buy me!" Eventually I find myself slowing down a little longer at a certain page. Finally, I narrow my choices to one quilt, often not a "wonderful" quilt, but a comfortable one. I just have to want to work with it.

Now I begin playing my favorite game—making several changes to the quilt that has inspired me in order to come up with a new quilt. Most antique quilts have no copyright, since most traditional patterns are now in the public domain. Many of today's quilts are protected by copyright, however, which means that those particular designs are owned by the quiltmakers or copyright holders and may not be reproduced. By using these quilts as my inspiration, however, and making several significant changes, I am creating my own design. Most often, my quilts hardly resemble the quilts which originally inspired them.

Even when a quilt is not copyrighted, the objective is still to make your own original designs. Getting into the habit of making your own design decisions will make your quilting experience more satisfying, and your quilts will be direct expressions of your own creativity.

What If . . . ?
Doors To Creativity

What If...? Doors to Creativity

❖ Understanding the elements of a quilt is essential to deciding what design changes you wish to make. The two basic elements of a quilt are color and pattern. Pattern itself can be subdivided into *block design, scale, set* and *borders.* Let's take a closer look at each of these elements.

COLOR

This refers not only to the obvious question of what colors are being used, but also to the color formula: *how* the colors are being used. Is it a scrap quilt, or was there a controlled number of fabrics in the quilt? How many different colors were used? How are the dark and light values positioned? What if you reversed them? This would create a change in coloration. A color-controlled quilt could be transformed into a scrap quilt. Changing the color formula is one of the simplest and easiest changes to make in any quilt design.

PATTERN

Block Design

What is the actual block pattern in the quilt that inspired you? Bear's Paw? Feathered Star? Shoo Fly? Could you change it to a similar, yet different block?

Scale

What is the size of the entire quilt? What are the dimensions of the borders and the sashing strips? What size block was used? Unless the actual dimensions are specified in the photo captions, it is impossible to know the actual size of the blocks. Therefore, when you draft your own templates, you are the one deciding on the size and scale of the blocks, sashings and borders. This is another change from the actual quilt.

Set

Was an adjacent, sashed, or alternating set used on the original quilt? Were the blocks set straight, or on the diagonal?

What if you added sashing where there was none? Or what if you eliminated sashing? How about alternating the blocks with a secondary connector block, rather than a solid square? Understanding the types of sets available makes it possible to create our own designs, based on existing quilts.

Borders

How many borders does the original quilt have? Are they pieced? Plain? Appliquéd? Are borders needed on your quilt? If the original quilt did not have any, what if you were to add them?

Making Your Original Quilt

Now that you understand the basic components of a quilt, it's time to begin. Use the worksheet provided on page 92 to guide you through the process. You are welcome to make several copies of it for your future use.

I suggest starting a notebook that contains a picture of the quilt that inspired you and any sketches, templates or drawings you made while working on the quilt. Also include a copy of the completed worksheet. This documentation will help you retrace the development of your own creative process. Any ideas you don't use in this quilt may be helpful with your next one.

The first question on the worksheet—where you found your picture—is a lot easier than the second—deciding what to change. Don't settle for reproducing someone else's vision, whether it's Grandma's century-old quilt, or a pattern purchased at a local quilt show. Use that antique quilt or purchased pattern as your inspiration and make some changes.

On the following pages, I will recount the creative process from original inspiration to new quilt. By following this path, you will feel comfortable employing similar techniques to create unique and original quilts.

Quilts &
Their Inspirations

Quilts & Their Inspirations

❖ Out of the blue, you'll recall someone's comment made months earlier. Because of your own experience, you now understand better what was meant. This happened to me years ago when I first started quilting. I attended a lecture where Jean Ray Laury spoke about the importance of working in series with your quilts. At the time, I couldn't understand how I could slow down and concentrate on making variations of the same quilt, when there were so many other quilts I wanted to experiment with for the first time. I remember raising my hand in the huge auditorium and asking Jean how this could be possible. In her wisdom gathered from experience she replied, "When the time is right, you will know it, and it will happen naturally."

Now, many quilts later, I understand what she meant. If you have ever felt the urge to see what would happen if you "rearranged the parts," then try further developing the design. This is the time when it will be "right . . . and it will happen naturally." The satisfaction of developing a quilt concept this way is incredible.

The following pages contain many examples of inspiring quilts with at least one derivation made by me or one of my students.

Single Irish Chain

1A

When my sister Cynthia announced her engagement, I wanted to make her a wedding quilt. I needed a "quick" quilt because the engagement was to be short. In Country Living magazine I found a beautiful antique red and white Single Irish Chain quilt. In this quilt, the blocks were set on point and alternated with solid squares and a triple border of two red strips separated by a center white strip.

I decided to make my quilt (quilt 1A) with the same set, number of blocks and triple border as the inspirational quilt. I used strip-piecing techniques to create quick nine-patch blocks. First, I determined the size and scale of the blocks and decided on six-inch blocks (change #1: scale). Then I transformed the color scheme to blue and white (change #2: color). I had no idea how the original quilt was quilted, so I designed my own quilting motif (change #3: quilting design).

While working on this quilt, I came up with other possibilities for the simple nine-patch blocks and soon found myself working "in series." For the second chain quilt I asked, "What if the blocks were set straight rather than on point?" Quilt 1B is the result.

1B

1C

Working with scraps whetted my appetite for working with different colorations. The possibilities in a series are infinite!

Then I wondered what the solid square would look like with stenciling and Quilt 1C came to life. This is a great "quick and easy" baby quilt. What if you used a delightful baby print or pre-printed panels in place of the stencilling?

Quilt 1D illustrates the use of "scrap" fabrics rather than the simple, two-color interpretation. I also scaled down the size of the nine-patch to three inches and added appliquéd hearts in some of the solid squares. A whimsical border seemed more appropriate than straight strips.

▶

1D

I wondered what it would look like if I used two different colors for the diagonal chain rows... and what if a third fabric were used where the chains crossed over, for a transparent look? After all, when blue and yellow paint are mixed, green is created. Why not do the same with fabric? Quilt 1E illustrates this effect. The blue prints run in one direction and the purple prints, in the other. Where they intersect, a purplish print suggests the overlapping of the two. This quilt also shows how effectively a few triangles can complement a pattern, and work as an integrated border.

▶

1E

1F

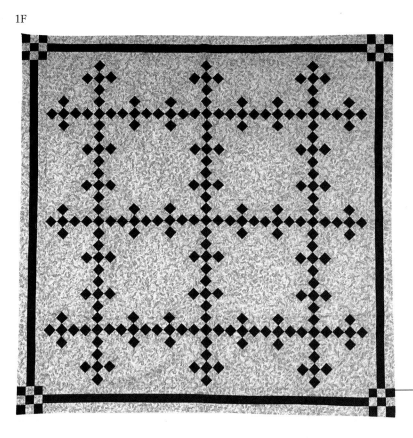

Quilt 1F is a Double Nine-Patch. You could start all over again with the same "what if's," this time working with a Double Nine-Patch. Or how about a Double Irish Chain? Or one made in scraps... on point... with appliqué in the solid block areas?

◀

▲

2

Rails and Fences

Quilt 2A emphasizes the illusion of interwoven strips—fabrics are consistent throughout the blocks of each diagonal row (change #1: coloration). Because I had no idea of the original quilt's size, I came up with my own (change #2: scale). The altered borders (change #3) and quilting design (change #4) also set this quilt apart from the antique quilt.

▼

After many of my students had requested that I teach the Rail Fence design, I wondered how to see "creativity" in it. The Rail Fence square is an arrangement of strips (any number) grading color from darkest to lightest. I define the Fence Post square as a group of strips arranged dark/light/dark or medium/light/medium. Because I had been looking for three-strip blocks, I paid closer attention to this old Fence Post design (quilt 2) in *Pieced Quilt: an American Tradition* by Jonathan Holstein. In this adaptation the coloration is dark/light/dark. The blocks are also set on point, which had never occurred to me. With this change in set and color, the blocks appear to be weaving over and under each other. This fascinated me.

My excitement about Rail Fence variations grew. I wondered, "What if I controlled the number of fabrics?" With quilt 2B, instead of using a scrap collection, I used one dark, one medium and one light fabric. This time the under/over "weave" truly showed up. I came up with many variations on this woven lattice theme, too many to illustrate here, but I will share one more example.

▶

2B

2C

Quilt 2C was made by Renee Charity. Renee used wonderful large-scale florals and sneaked a strip of golden fabric into the strip-piecing. What a perfect example of transforming a traditional pattern into a powerful piece of abstract quilt art! Much of today's quilt art is firmly rooted in traditional quilt patterns, but with innovative fabrics and a few surprise "spices," who can tell what will happen next?

▶

Bow Ties

3

▲

The Bow Tie pattern appears in numerous publications and quilt collections. I particularly liked one that I saw in the home of Christiane Meunier. Christiane's Bow Tie quilt (3) would have been easy for me to copy color for color and line for line, but that would have been too predictable and not much fun.

I decided to keep the Bow Tie block and simplified it by eliminating the set-in piecing and using strip-piecing techniques (change #1: pattern). While it is indeed a Bow Tie, "Too Many Ties" (3A) is in a different arrangement. I worked with a common background and a broad scrappy palette of fabrics and colors including black, green, red, purple, blue, and brown (change #2: color). I quickly made the blocks and designed the set on my flannel wall. (See page 60 for a discussion of using the flannel wall for designing purposes.) I began arranging and rearranging the blocks until I liked the results. Notice that the Fields and Furrows set (in the manner of Log Cabin quilts) was followed in the final arrangement. Diagonal rows of color across the surface of the quilt added strength to the random coloration in the blocks (change #3: set).

▶

3A

3B

Quilt 3B resulted from blocks left over from quilt 3A. Working and designing on a flannel wall, I frequently have extra blocks. What if the blocks were set on point? What if a scrappy "bits-and-pieces" border were used on the quilt? The more you get into this "what if" concept of working with quilts, the more like eating potato chips it becomes—you can't stop at one!

◀

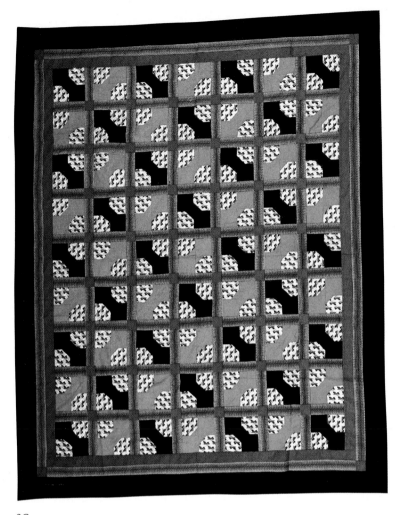

3C

> *I frequently have extra blocks. I like to think of these as "planned overs" rather than leftovers, and they often become a great start for another quilt!*

3D

Quilt 3C was made by Linda Packer. In this quilt, Linda wanted to see what would happen if a controlled set of fabrics were used rather than a scrap collection. She made both black and blue ties, each with a common background fabric, placed blue ties diagonally in one direction and black in the other. What if the blocks were sashed? The set is so dynamic in this quilt, it's difficult to see the Bow Tie block!

Quilt 3D, also by Linda Packer, is made from a pastel palette of fabrics. Instead of associating the pattern with a man's bow tie, we now see soft baby bows. Associating color with an emotional response is something we don't often think about with quilts, even though color is usually the first thing we respond to.

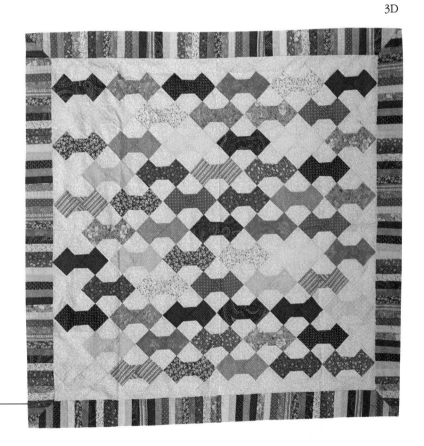

Double Irish Chain

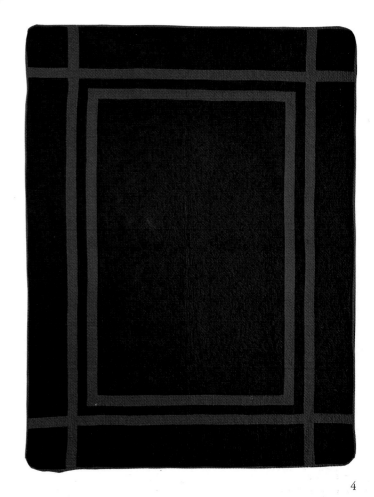

4

Why do some quilters feel the need to finish one project completely before starting another? They probably remember their mothers telling them to finish one task before starting the next. I honestly believe that quilts turn out better if there is some time between start and finish. Often it's not in the quilt's best interest to rush the process. Take your time in making decisions. I had been working on a Double Irish Chain quilt at the time I was reading *Quilts from the Indiana Amish*. I was immediately drawn to this quilt (4) because the border seemed to glow in the dark. This border was the one I wanted for my Double Irish Chain.

▶

4A

With the addition of this special border, I created a unique variation (4A) of a familiar traditional pattern.

▶

5

Ohio Star

The soothing brown and blue tones of the antique Sawtooth Star quilt (5) pictured in an issue of Lady's Circle Patchwork Quilts give this quilt a feeling of serenity. I loved the brown stars on the muslin background and knew I wanted to work with this quilt.

◀

Using an Ohio Star block in my quilt (5A) instead of the Sawtooth Star was easy enough (change #1: pattern). My color formula was brown stars on a muslin background, and the Ohio Star allowed me to use a third color (change #2). I decided to make each star from different brown and lavender fabrics. I could find only a handful of lavender fabrics, and was forced to "stretch" the color palette to include pink, rose, peach, and coral fabrics for each star. I pieced the blocks together over several months. When I had enough made, I was ready to begin designing on my flannel wall. Instead of duplicating the original quilt by setting my Ohio Stars with solid squares of blue fabric, I tried a tangent set, a sashed set, diagonal blocks, connector blocks, etc. Suddenly it occurred to me that it didn't have to be all one way. What if I combined an alternating set with a tangent set? Satisfying my need to have the same emotional response each time I looked at the original quilt, I used the blue squares. As I became more and more excited, I couldn't sew fast enough to get the blocks together. The border practically created itself— where the star points came together, sparkling diamonds seemed to leap from the surface of the quilt. Repeating that same line in the border seemed the perfect final touch.

▶

5A

Quilt 5B shows how Debbie McCarter responded to my quilt. Debbie used the same block in a tangent set throughout. She even made use of the same border-pieced unit. Look carefully! Even though the piecing structure is identical, it looks entirely different, due to the coloration.

►

Quilt 5C was the result of a fund-raising quilt which I coordinated in 1985. Patterns for six-inch Ohio Star blocks were distributed to quilters around San Diego County, but blocks arrived from across the nation. Anyone interested was asked to piece an Ohio Star block using muslin for the background, dark tones for the center square and star points, and medium tones for the inner accent triangles. When over 300 blocks came in, I wondered if I had created a monster! The blocks were very disparate: the color of the muslin ranged from true beige to glaring white; the quality of the fabrics, from cheese-cloth to canvas.

5B

5C

Fortunately, I had no particular set in mind prior to beginning the design phase on the flannel wall. I sorted the blocks first by size; anything that wasn't exactly six inches was set aside. Then I sorted by color. I can't tell you how many arrangements I tried before deciding on blue squares. There would be no mistaking "Legacy Star Quilt" for the original… still there is definitely a family resemblance!

◄

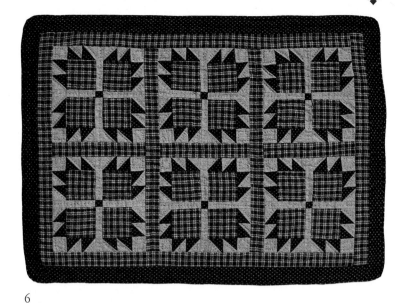

6

▲

Bear's Paw

The creative process should never be rushed. Quilts, like wine, need to age and ripen with time.

This miniature Bear's Paw quilt (6) in Cabin Fever Calicoes' catalog inspired the next series of quilts. I liked the beige and navy blue colors, as well as the plaid fabric.

6A

In quilt 6A, I drafted my own patterns and automatically made a scale change. Next, I worked with the color formula. The original was a color-controlled quilt with one beige, a blue/beige plaid and a blue print. A scrappy effect was created with varying shades of beige for the background of each block, shades of navy blue for the "toes" and a plaid for the "paw." Whereas the original quilt was composed of only six blocks, I made nine. I also used a tangent set, rather than a sashed set, which made the triangular toes of adjacent blocks merge to create another pattern. Once again, the borders seemed to have a life of their own. I coordinated them with the rest of the quilt by repeating the scrappy combinations from the blocks. It is to branch out and change the very elements of the antique quilt that attracted you in the first place. However, think of all the advantages we have over our grandmothers who had no quilt magazines, quilt shows or classes to inspire them!

◀

The following Bear's Paw quilts show what could happen to the same block if the blocks were colored positively and negatively. Quilt 6B is composed of only two fabrics; this coloration is rarely seen today. It's sometimes called a Robbing Peter to Pay Paul interpretation, and can be used on many patterns. I call this my UCLA Bruins quilt because the inner border looks like cheerleaders somersaulting down the field!

▶

6B

Quilt 6C illustrates what happens when a Log Cabin Fields and Furrows set is used. With this in mind, Cheryl Morris created this pink and blue Baby Bear's Paw quilt. She worked out the colors of each block on graph paper to determine exactly how many all-blue, all-pink and half-pink/half-blue blocks were needed—this can be done for any quilt.

6C

▶

6D

One way to enlarge a small quilt is by putting the blocks on point and alternating them with solid squares, as Linda Sawry did in quilt 6D. It takes fewer blocks for a given quilt size when the blocks are set diagonally. This is a good trick to remember when making bed-sized quilts.

◀

6E

Sandi Justice made her quilt (6E) a bit smaller than Linda's by putting her blocks on point in a tangent set and filling the remaining space with half-square triangles.

A quilt can also be made larger simply by adding cornerstones and sashing, as Sharon Kostink did in quilt 6F.

▲

6F

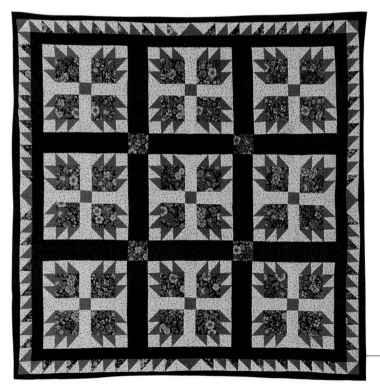

◀

Pine Tree

This antique Pine Tree quilt by Ettie Ellen Brees (7) in *Quilts and Quilters of Illinois* by Rita Barber impressed me and I wanted to work with this design.

▶

7

7A

▲

Jean Tebo's modern-day interpretation of the Pine Tree design (7B) is unlike the antique quilt because she divided the block design. All of her pine trees point in the same direction and are made from both printed and solid fabrics.

▼

7B

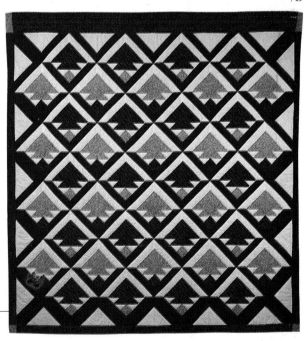

In Quilt 7A I chose to stay with the original block and selected a 10 1/2" block to change the scale. I decided on an alternating diagonal set, but instead of the solid squares I designed a secondary connector block which featured floating green squares. I also changed the color formula from a red and white format to various greens and ecru colors. I used one ecru in the Pine Tree blocks, but the connector block and border incorporate several tone-on-tone ecru prints. Imagine this quilt done in wild, brilliant fabrics to create a totally different explosion of color.

8A

▲

Terrific Triangles

━━━

I found a beautiful antique triangle quilt in Better Homes and Garden's *American Patchwork and Quilting*. Looking at this quilt, I realized that I had never succeeded at making a quilt look "old" using today's fabrics. I set out to trick the viewer into thinking that my quilt was 100 years old. In order to achieve the look of the original quilt, I needed a wide palette of fabrics and colors.

I discovered how to combine fabrics, colors, and the scale of prints to create that rich patina of age. When I first began cutting triangles, the brown, black, and beige tones fell flat and I discovered that the original quilt actually needed blue, green, red, black and gray to give off that warm glow. Although Terrific Triangles #1 (8A) looks very similar to the antique quilt, I still managed to work in many changes. Besides the scale, I changed the corners and inserted a brick-colored border between the triangles and the striped border.

Quilt 8B, made of leftover triangles, resulted from a decision to work with the pattern, or line, of the quilt. I recognized Log Cabin elements (a square divided diagonally, half-light, half-dark). Any arrangement you can do with Log Cabin blocks can also be done with simple half-square triangles. I decided to add a different border treatment to give it a new look. Comparing these two quilts it is difficult to believe that they use exactly the same triangles.

▶

8B

By the time I made quilt 8C, I was ready to imprint my personal style. Wanting people to associate the quilt with me, I used my favorite color and pattern—green and the Medallion Star. Most patchwork blocks can be broken down into half-square triangles. Although a square may be what one immediately sees, it can be constructed with triangles. Keeping that in mind, I began with the star in the center and framed it with pieced triangles and the illusion of a twisting ribbon border. This time, I wanted there to be no mistaking my quilt for an old one! Because antique scrap quilts relied heavily on using a large variety of fabrics, I used a controlled palette for my 1980s scrap quilt, which is more typical of today's quilts.

▶

8C

8D

Quilt 8D is a charm quilt; no two fabrics are repeated. I had lots of fun playing with triangles and wanted to try another star pattern. This time I chose to repeat the star blocks, and every triangle was on the flannel wall before starting to sew them together. In all, 800 different fabrics were used. That represents a lot of fabric trading!

◀

8E

▲

Without doubt, quilt 8F (my token abstract) was my most difficult design. My quilts are firmly rooted in tradition, and here I ventured into unfamiliar territory. While growing as quiltmakers, we sometimes experience uncomfortable, even unpleasant feelings. However, there is truth to the expression, "No pain, no gain." I'd always had high expectations for my students, and felt I had to push myself, as well. Again, I turned to my books for visual stimulation and found direction in Roberta Horton's *Calico and Beyond*. Work with a line! This quilt is called "A-Maze-ing." If you look closely at this quilt, you'll notice the line of dark triangles begins in the upper left-hand corner and continues along in maze-like fashion, ending in the lower right-hand corner. I'm not sure whether it's more incredible that the quilt forms a maze or that I finally succeeded in creating an abstract art quilt! Either way, the result was worth the agony. I *love* this quilt!

▼

Quilt 8E is my attempt to work with Terrific Triangles in an Amish mode. Once again, I turned to the visual stimulation in books and magazines to settle on a pattern which looked truly Amish. One of the things which makes Amish quilts work the way they do is the wide range of fabrics in them. Over 40 different solid-colored fabrics and eight different blacks are used in this quilt. I counted navy blue and gray among the blacks.

8F

One Patch

One of my students, Emily Packer, selected this old linsey-woolsey quilt (9) from *Homage to Amanda* by Edwin Binney, 3rd and Gail Binney-Winslow as her inspiration. I couldn't imagine how Emily was inspired by this design, and when she brought in the ugliest fabric I had ever seen, I could only hope that she hadn't paid much for it. However, not wanting to hamper her creativity, I kept such thoughts to myself.

▶

9

When she brought in the finished quilt top (9A), I was floored! Although many beautiful quilts are the products of my classes, it's an especially rare one that I covet. Emily's quilt is one of these. This little quilt totally captivates me and has taught me a valuable lesson at the same time. Students aren't the only ones who do the learning.

Emily created a contemporary look by making an irregularly shaped quilt with extremely bright colors. The squares seem to pulsate into the border, which appears to be an urban landscape. We tend to get caught in a rut at times and are always drawn to the same colors, the same type of fabrics and the same type of quilts. What if we chose something a little bit different? Remember Christal Carter's definition of creativity—the willingness to be a little different.

◀

Ocean Waves

10

*My challenge for this quilt was
to work with exactly the same block,
color palette and fabric type, while
making an unmistakably
contemporary quilt*

I can still remember the first time I saw this whimsical Ocean Waves baby quilt (10) in the 1984 *Quilt Engagement Calendar*. When I opened the page to this quilt, I gasped in awe. I know in my heart that it isn't a wonderful quilt, but it has a magical quality that made me want to work with it. As usual, I started by drafting my own templates and decided on a six-inch block (change #1: scale). I spent most of one day selecting fabrics and cutting pieces. From each fabric, I cut enough pieces for half of one block and stored them in a box labelled "Ocean Waves Variation."

◀

Whenever I had some spare time, I stitched a few blocks together and deliberately made no attempt to match the fabrics—I actually closed my eyes to select them! When I had a box full of completed blocks, I experimented with the Log Cabin format on the flannel wall. I realized, once again, that the block was similar to a Log Cabin—divided diagonally, half light and half dark. I played with the various possibilities of Fields and Furrows, Barn Raising, and other light and dark variations. It wasn't until I tried grouping colors (change #1) that I felt the quilt advance into the 20th century—fulfilling my original challenge. Changing the set (change #2) and adding a border (change #3) also helped update it. The quilt is named "Creativity in Motion" (10A) because I believe that the triangular shapes capture the glimmer of rippling water. One student, however, suggested the even more appropriate name, "Shimmering Triangles," because the vibrant colors appear to be dancing beneath the water's surface.

▼

10A

LeMoyne Stars

I found quilt 11 in the book *Treasury of American Quilts* by Cyril Nelson and Carter Houck. It enticed me to begin a scrap LeMoyne Star project.

◀

Once again, I used a box for this ongoing project. Inside it, I placed diamonds cut from many different fabrics and muslin to be used for the background. When a class presented me with a box of nine red and green Snow Crystal blocks, I merged them with my star blocks to make a larger quilt than the Snow Crystal blocks would allow. To complement the 12" block, a three-strip sashing composed of green fabric between two strips of muslin (11A) was made. The muslin strips appear to merge with the similarly colored background of the block. To create more visual interest, an appliquéd border that repeated the diamond-shaped flowers and leaves was added. I named this quilt "Starlight Express."

▶

Now I needed an idea for the many stars still left in the box! So I searched through my books and pictures and found inspiration in the Jeanette Lasansky book *Pieced by Mother* (11B) and everything flowed from there.

►

11C

11B

Instead of a Lone Star for the medallion center, I selected a 24" Feathered Star for quilt 11C, simply because I'm partial to them. I drafted many possibilities on graph paper prior to starting the flannel wall stage of designing this quilt. I don't usually start this way, but in order to give the feeling of stars floating on the surface, it was easier to establish a structure first. With the exception of four five-inch LeMoyne Stars in the corners of the Feathered Star, all of the stars were already made and waiting in the box. I call this quilt "Stars, Stars and More Stars."

◄

12

Sawtooth
Baskets

When Linda Hamby saw this quilt (12) by Margaret Steele Entrekin in Jeanette Lasansky's book *Pieced by Mother,* she immediately wanted to work with it. Enamored by the soft pastel palette and the simple basket block, Linda chose to stay with these same elements. But, how could she make an original quilt?

◀

12A

Linda drafted her own pieces on a different scale, and while playing with the blocks on the flannel wall, noticed similarities between the basket block and the Log Cabin block. Using that feature, she began arranging blocks in common Log Cabin arrangements: Barn Raising, Light and Dark variation, Fields and Furrows, etc. Linda finally settled on Fields and Furrows and took it one step further by grouping her blocks in diagonal rows according to color (12A). Many old patterns attract us with their whimsical arrangements and can be updated by playing with the pattern.

▶

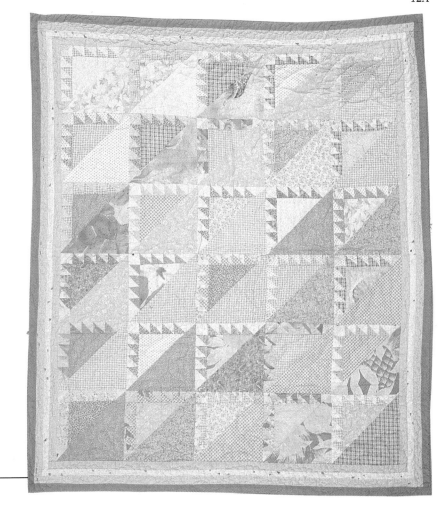

Feathered Stars

13

13A

▲

Marsha McCloskey's book *Feathered Star Quilts* presents a multitude of design possibilities. Her "Christmas Banner" (13) masterfully combines three Feathered Stars and pieced borders. This quilt made the illusive seem obvious.

I mentioned earlier how much I love to make Feathered Stars. I also teach classes on the drafting and construction of Feathered Stars, and after a few of these classes, ended up with three identical brown and green blocks. By then I was out of the green background fabric. I really liked the combination and wanted to do something special with these three orphan blocks—what use could be made of three blocks and no more background fabric?

With Marsha's quilt as the catalyst, I made quilt 13A with the three class blocks and some pieced borders. Sometimes borrowing one element is enough to get you going on your own design. Thank you, Marsha!

▶

Pineapple Log Cabin

The Pineapple Log Cabin quilt is usually associated with an overall design, with the same block repeated again and again.

Ione Skaar's modern adaptation of the Pineapple Log Cabin is pure genius. She was inspired by Charlotte Ballard's Pineapple quilt (14) in the book, *Pineapple Passion,* by Nancy Smith and Lynda Milligan.

Ione wanted a small Christmas wallhanging and chose colors accordingly. She designed the red poinsettias in the corners to frame the Pineapple block (14A). Here's a wonderful way of trying out a pattern without embarking on a huge project. Think about the possibilities! Time may no longer stand between you and all those other quilts you've wanted to make.

Medallions

Deborah Timby's "Stars Over Hawaii" quilt (15) inspired me at a time when I really needed it. I had committed myself to making a medallion quilt, but at that time there weren't any books or articles about them. I could only stare at pictures of old and new medallion quilts and try to evaluate what I did and didn't like about each one.

▶

◀ **M**aking my medallion quilt (15A) was a slow and painful process. I wanted to set my medallion center on point, but this created large triangles, and I don't like large empty spaces on medallion quilts. How would I fill them?

Deborah's quilt provided me with the answer. She had divided the triangles with bars of color that seemed almost three-dimensional, drawing the eye outward from the center and all over the quilt. A successful medallion distributes its weight evenly throughout the quilt; no one area is too strong. Using this same concept, I experimented with fabrics and colors until hitting upon a combination which felt right, and distributed these same fabrics symmetrically throughout the rest of the quilt for balance. The contrasting fabrics within and around the star created a pulsating effect.

Sisterhood

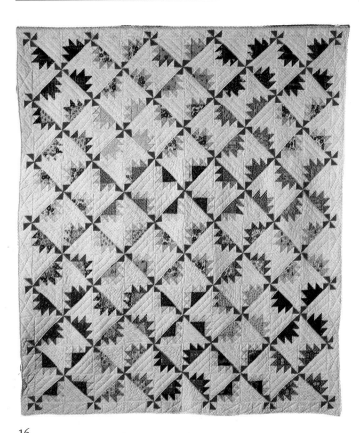

Alvia Troutt's Kansas Troubles quilt (16) has bright red triangles that give the effect of tiny whirling pinwheels all over her quilt. The block which I selected is actually 1/4 of a block, and it looks very similar to Kansas Troubles. This was just one of the patterns offered to my students on signature quilts. Students learn to develop their own ways of seeing patterns, which in turn leads to greater creativity in their finished quilts. The Sisterhood series reflects that creativity. It wasn't until the end of the class series when students came with finished quilt tops that I realized how much fun this little block could be! I think it is impossible to recognize the original block in some of the quilts.

◀

16

16A

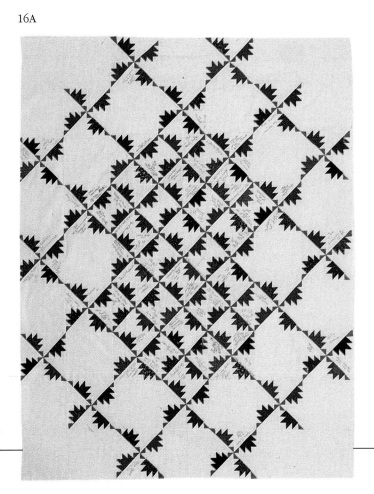

I grouped four of the blocks together into a pinwheel configuration in my quilt (16A), coloring the end triangles red to make the extra pinwheel. Originally, I had intended to make the entire quilt like the center, in a tangent set. But when I arranged the blocks that way on the flannel wall, it seemed too busy, and the quilt would also have been too small (I used four-inch blocks). The alternating set of solid squares made the quilt larger, and calmer.

◀

Donna Baker and Sandy Anderson chose to work with the Barn Raising concept based on a Log Cabin block arrangement. Donna's elegant variation (16B) has a straight set and in the four sections of the quilt, the colored half of each block faces the center. The pieced border adds a feeling of motion to her design.

▶

16B

Sandy's Sisterhood blocks are set on point (16C). With the blocks pointing outward, she created the effect of three-dimensional overlapping squares.

◀

16D

16C

Becky Zorn used her blocks to frame a church (16D). The surrounding blocks are placed in an interesting variation of the Barn Raising set. She made this quilt as a presentation gift for her son's youth pastor to commemorate her son's confirmation; each of the students in his confirmation class signed one of the blocks.

▶

16E

*I provide students with line drawings
of quilt blocks, with no indication of
where darks or lights should be
placed or how many
different fabrics should be used.*

16F

▲

Louise Hixon created a wonderful star effect in her quilt (16E). How did she do that? The illusion is that the blocks are set on point, with extra triangles whimsically attached. Not so! They are placed in a straight, tangent set.

The original block design is difficult to recognize in Kris Zook's quilt (16F), too. She used a scrap coloration with the larger triangle at the bottom of the block in a dark value to match the little triangles at the top. Setting the blocks on point and turning them randomly gives a very different effect.

▶

Confetti

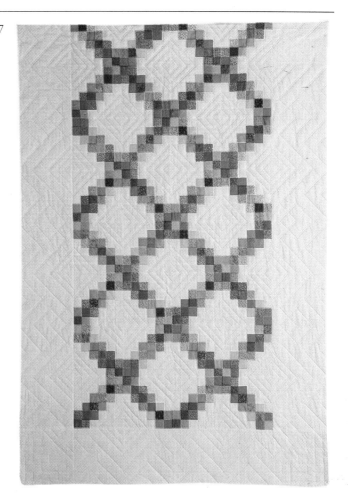

17

When I saw Elizabeth Croy's delightful "Confetti" scrap quilt (17) in an issue of *Traditional Quiltworks* magazine, I immediately converted this pattern to strip-piecing methods. The biggest decision was how to color the block. The possibilities are endless!

▶

17A

▲ Linda Packer used rich jewel tones to create the overlapping color effect in her Confetti quilt (17A). The black lattice creates strong contrast, while the fabric in the cornerstones echoes one of the colors used in the chain. (See page 60 for Confetti block and other designs on a flannel wall.)

My confetti quilt (17B) has a control fabric in the background, which is repeated in the center of the chain. In one direction, the outer chain fabric is a solid color, while a print is placed in the other direction giving this quilt a look of interwoven chains floating across a light background. ▶

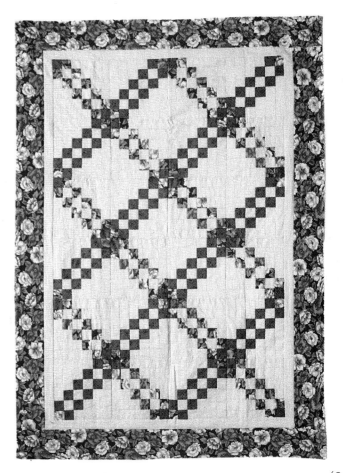

17B

49

Attic Windows

This was another project first designed for my adult education classes. I had avoided using this block because the design seemed too static, but then one day I saw something besides the obvious window—I saw a directional unit. As shown in Judy Florence's book, *Award-Winning Scrap Quilts*, careful attention to color value in her quilt (18) creates rays of light that sparkle directionally—across the surface of her Attic Window variation. Once I forced myself to think beyond the obvious value placements in sill, sash and pane, the design possibilities truly opened up. The following quilts range from very traditional to, "You're kidding—that can't possibly be an Attic Window!" But I promise, they are!

◀

18

18A

I reversed the traditional positions of the light and dark values in quilt 18A. Arranging these blocks on the flannel wall helped to achieve a strongly diagonal design—ribbons or streamers seem to twist across the surface of this quilt. Asymmetrical borders work with the design to create a very non-tradtional quilt.

◀

Carol O'Brien created windows of different sizes to frame the darling cat panels she had been saving for just the right quilt (18B).

▶

18B

18C

Laurine Leeke's quilt (18C) definitely does not resemble Attic Windows! Her variation demonstrates that, when sash and sill values are the same, the flat window units become a new design element. Don't you love the sparkle added by the stars?

◀

18D

In quilt 18D I experimented by setting the blocks on point and turning some of them a quarter-turn to create a unique look. This quilt always amazes me. It started out as a demo quilt in a class. I don't think I really expected to finish it, but once I began playing with arrangements on the flannel wall and losing the feeling of the window, the result fascinated me. Who says the Attic Window can't be set on point?

▶

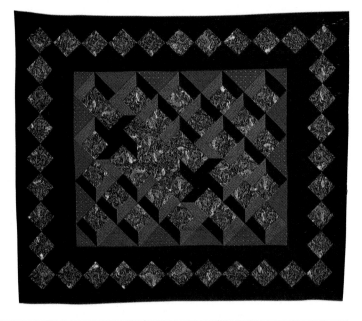

Pyramids Plus

Anything that can be done with 60° diamonds can also be done with pyramid units.

19

In preparing for my Thousand Pyramids class, I asked students to contribute strips for my quilt without telling them what kind of quilt it was to be. A few students helped me test the idea of team-building the units, and by the time the units were made for this quilt (19A), I was hooked!

▼

This Thousand Pyramids quilt from Jonathan Holstein's *Pieced Quilt: An American Tradition,* is a showcase of wonderful fabrics and colors. For years I avoided this pattern because I didn't think it lent itself to creativity. And besides, I hated the idea of cutting all those equilateral triangles. I decided to work with this design, however, when I stumbled upon the concept of unit sewing in one of Sara Nephew's books.

◄

19B

My "Diamond Design" quilt (19B) is another variation. In this pattern you can truly see the diamond-shaped design created with the pyramid units. The bonus is that it's all straight-seam sewing, whereas most diamond patterns have some set-in pieces.

◀

19C

Sandy Andersen's Baby Blocks variation (19C) illustrates straight-seam sewing well. To achieve this design, you must have three values: dark, medium and light; without the proper contrast, the Baby Block design is not visible. In Sandy's quilt, the three-dimensional blocks seem to float against the inner border, while the middle and outer borders frame her quilt.

◀

New quilters don't have the stockpile of fabrics required for that "old" Thousand Pyramids effect, which led me to wonder what would happen if I controlled the colors. It takes four strips of the same color to create pyramid units of a given color. This pink and green quilt (19D) shows my first attempt at controlled color. I made light pink, light green and dark green units and alternated them. No two units are exactly alike, but each is made with the same prints.

▶

19D

19E

Another pyramids possibility is the hexagon shape. Laurine Leeke realized that she could create a secondary star pattern by varying the pyramid unit slightly. Instead of making the unit entirely in one color or value, Laurine put a white triangle inside three black triangles. She threw in a little red for spice and made a great quilt (19E)!

▶

Another of Laurine's quilts (19F) works well in value without regard to color. There are a lot of colors represented, but the values are truly dark in the dark position and truly light in the light position. She began with the Barn Raising set and played with arrangements on the flannel wall until she discovered the design she liked best.

◀

19F

19G

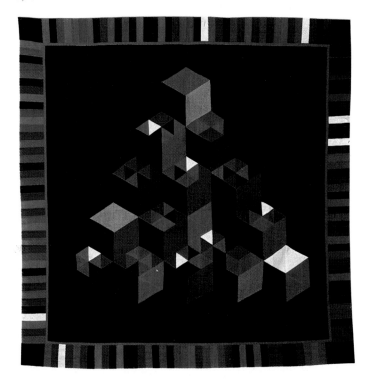

Patty Barney's quilt is another great design made up of 60° diamond shapes. She worked with smaller units, all solids, and a few scattered white triangles to create an electric feeling in her Thousand Pyramids variation (19G). The striking color combination makes this a very dramatic quilt.

◀

Hawaiian Flag

Emily Packer was soon ready to start her next quilt, and I didn't bat an eye when she brought in the picture of the Hawaiian Flag quilt (20) from *Quilt Digest* #2. Anyone capable of bringing such whimsy to the old linsey-woolsey quilt can do almost anything. (See page 37)

▶

20

20A

I just love Emily's wild elephant interpretation (20A). The Hawaiian Flag quilt is clearly its source of inspiration; this quilt reflects Emily's fresh, innovative approach.

◀

Now It's Your Turn

Now It's Your Turn

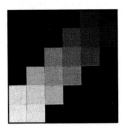

Figure 1

Figure 2

Figure 3

Figure 1 is the basic block. Figures 2-6 show some different flannel wall combinations.

❖ This book is not a "how-to" manual. There are many good books about the technical aspects of quilting. My goal is to take you beyond the basics of how to select fabrics and cut pieces. If you still want help in these areas, check the Suggested Reading list at the back of this book.

The most important thing to do in designing and creating your own quilts is simply to begin! With your workspace prepared and your mind open, willing and eager, you can find a wealth of visual stimulation in books, calendars and magazines. Choose a photo of a quilt you want to work with, fill in the worksheet and you're ready to start!

Draft Templates

After coming up with an original design, the next step is to draft your own pattern pieces. I think this is one of the most crucial steps in making quilts that are "yours." If you have never drafted your own pattern pieces, it's time to learn how! Check local quilt shops for a class in basic pattern drafting, or read *Traditional Quiltworks* magazine's regular feature on drafting.

Select Fabrics

This is the really fun part—and don't worry about making mistakes! Even "mistakes" can be used in a quilt, and we can often learn a lot from making them!

Spend some time really looking at quilts and decide what you like about them and what you don't like. Once you understand the things that please you, it will be much easier to incorporate them into your own quilts. If you recognize that you really hate quilts in a certain shade of purple, you will know to avoid using that color in your quilts.

Get Your Flannel Wall Ready

When your patterns are drafted, fabrics selected, pieces cut and blocks completed, you'll be ready to design your quilt on a flannel wall (Figures 1-6). Because cotton fabrics cling to it without pins or tape, your quilt blocks can be moved around easily. Furthermore, working on a wall is much easier than bending over or kneeling on the floor, and it also keeps pets, children and spouses away from your work in progress.

If you can't devote an entire wall to flannel, improvise! How about using a closet door, or a refrigerator? A good friend of mine purchased an artist's canvas and wrapped flannel around it and stapled it into place. The canvas can stand on a couch, lean against a window, and even hang temporarily on a wall with push pins. It is also portable enough to take to workshops.

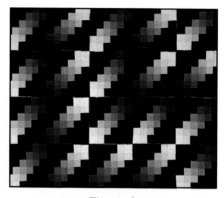

Figure 4

Explore Setting Possibilities

This is playtime! What if you set the blocks straight, or in an adjacent set? How about a diagonal set or alternating the blocks with solid squares? How about sashing? Could it be straight or diagonal? Pieced or appliquéd? Remember, it doesn't have to be "all or nothing." You can combine types of sets and borders in one quilt. Try using a set which you have never made before—how about a typical Amish "bars" set? (My own personal challenge is to avoid using the adjacent set again and again.)

Figure 5

Choose a Border

The creative decisions you make will not end with the body of the quilt. You still have to decide on the borders and the quilting. Just start sewing, and make your decisions as you go. Borders can be as simple or as complex as you choose. Some quilts cry out for elaborately pieced borders. My "Feathered Star Medley" quilt (#13A, page 43) needed all of those pieced borders to frame it, while "Creativity in Motion" (#10 A, page 39) definitely needed to be calmed down by the use of simple, striped borders.

Think of a quilt as you would a painting. Some paintings require very simple frames, or even a plastic or Lucite™ box, which adds no further statement to the piece. On the other hand,

Figure 6

Not only is experimenting on flannel walls fun, it also reaps creative rewards.

some paintings require elaborate matting, or ornate gilt frames. It will be the same with your quilts. The type of border you select will make a statement for the whole quilt.

Quilt the Top

"How should I quilt my quilt?" is probably the second most commonly asked question I hear. (The question I am asked most often is, "How much fabric should I buy?") I'll tell you what I tell my adult education students—I don't know how you should quilt your quilts! I tend to see straight, geometric lines on all of my quilts, while my friend Arlene sees curves on hers. I love what quilted curves "say" on Arlene's quilts, but curves don't "feel" right on mine. Remember that this is one of the creative decisions we each have to make—trust your own creative impulses and do what feels right for you!

Keep an Open Mind

As a teacher, I like to be very careful about setting strict rules. I often remind students that rules should be considered as guidelines. If you feel that they hinder your creativity, bend them a bit! If you like the way something looks, go with it and rely on your own judgement. There are few absolutely right or wrong decisions, only what pleases you and what does not. Do you think that Grandma worried about all those details? Do you think she might have stopped working on a quilt because no one had told her exactly which border design to use, or how to quilt the top? Of course not—and the same applies to you! Keep your creative doors open. What if you changed the set, the coloration, the sashing, the number and style of the borders? You would be creating your own, original quilt!

The patterns in the following pages are meant to be starting places for developing your own creativity. Even though certain measurements, yardage and pattern pieces are given, don't feel limited by the text or the pictures in this book. Remember that it is okay to start small and build on that—you're limited only by your own imagination. Plunge right in and have fun!

What If . . . ?
Design Challenges

General Directions for Cutting Strips

❖ All fabric should be washed and pressed. Fold 44"-45" fabric in half, selvage to selvage, keeping the fold even and flat. (The raw edges may be somewhat uneven.) Fold the fabric in half once more. This creates four layers of fabric, approximately 11" wide (Figure 1).

Position the folded fabric on a cutting mat. I prefer mats that have grids because the grid lines ensure that my strips will be straight, without "bends" at each fold. Two things cause bends in fabric strips. The first is folding fabric unevenly and the second is an incorrect angle of the ruler in relationship to the folds of the fabric. The ruler must be absolutely perpendicular to the folds, or there will be bends in your cut strips.

Line up the fold of the fabric with one of the horizontal lines on your cutting mat, approximately 3" up from the bottom edge of the mat. Right-handed people should position the fabric so that it extends to the right. Left-handed people should position the fabric so that it extends to the left (Figure 2).

Align the ruler with one of the vertical grid lines and you will make perpendicular cuts. Note: if your cutting mat does not have grid lines, you can draw two lines on it with a fine-point permanent marker or pen. The first line should be 3" up from the bottom edge of the mat and the second line should be 3" in from the left side of the mat. (Reverse this line if you are left handed.)

Begin by eliminating the uneven edges of the fabric, as shown in Figure 3. Place the ruler just over the uneven edges of the fabric, aligning it with a vertical line on the mat. Hold the rotary cutter at a 45° angle to the cutting mat. Make a clean cut through the fabric, beginning in front of the fold of the fabric and cutting through the fabric to the opposite edge with one clean stroke of the cutter (no short, choppy strokes). Always cut away from yourself—*never* toward yourself!

Move the ruler to the proper position for cutting the first strip of fabric and continue to cut strips until you have the required number. Always move the ruler, not the fabric. This will help keep the cut edges even. To make sure that your strips are straight, open up one fabric strip and check the spots where there were folds. If the fabric was not evenly lined up or the ruler was incorrectly positioned, there will be a bend at each of the folds in the fabric as shown (Figure 4).

When cutting many strips, check after every four or five strips to make sure the strips are straight. Leave the other strips folded in fourths until you are ready to use them.

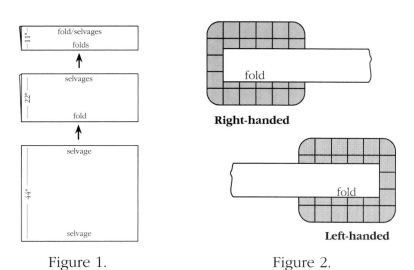

Figure 1.   Figure 2.

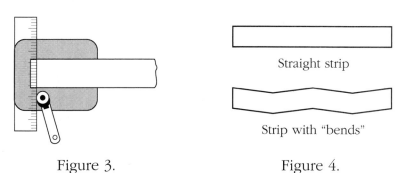

Figure 3.   Figure 4.

What If...? Bear's Paw

quilts shown on pages 30-32

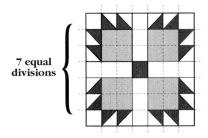

7 equal divisions

Figure 1.

❖ Most quilt historians agree that the Bear's Paw is a pattern that dates back to the early days of America, when pioneers had to stake their claim against nature. In western Pennsylvania and Ohio it was called Bear's Paw, while the Quakers of Philadelphia called it "Hand of Friendship." And quilters on Long Island knew this pattern by the name of "Duck's Foot in the Mud." In any case, the Bear's Paw pattern has stood the test of time, remaining a favorite block among quilters today. In some of the oldest Bear's Paw quilts it is not unusual to find that some of the "toes" have been turned backwards. Quilters often included such "planned" mistakes in their quilts because of the belief that only God could create something perfect.

The Bear's Paw block is based on a seven-patch grid. This means that the block is divided into seven equal divisions across and down the block (Figure 1). In this exercise, each division will be equal to 1", resulting in a 7" finished block. (If you would like to make your blocks a different size, just give each division another measurement. For example, a 1/2" division would result in a 3 1/2" finished block, a 1 1/2" division would give you a 10 1/2" block and a 2" division would make a 14" block.)

This design will allow you much room for creativity, especially in coloring your quilt. You'll need rotary cutting equipment for the speed techniques, but templates have been provided on page 90 (for 7" and 10 1/2" blocks) if you prefer traditional piecing. Bias strip piecing will be used to construct the "toes" for the Bear's Paw.

The following options are some of the ways you might choose to color your quilt. Numerous other colorations will probably occur to you as you sew, so jot down your ideas for future creations and have fun making your first Bear's Paw quilt.

• Option #1:

To make the quilt in only two fabrics (i.e. one light and one dark fabric), you will need approximately one yard of each fabric.

66

• Option #2:

This variation has dark "paws" and uses a different light for the background of each block. Also, the quilt has a light framing border that is different from all of the other lights used. To make this quilt, you will need 1/4 yard each of 10 different light-value fabrics, 1/4 yard of two darks (one for the "foot pad" and one for the "toe") *or* 1/2 yard of one dark (for both the "foot pad" and the "toe").

• Option #3:

Another possibility for the light position might be to use two different lights. For this, you will need 1/4 yard each of two lights and 1/4 yard of two darks (one for the "foot pad" and for the "toe") *or* 1/2 yard of one dark (for both).

The yardage given includes enough for borders. The "toes" of the Bear's Paw could be a different dark in each block. If you decide to do this, allow 1/4 yard of each dark.

If you decide to follow the more traditional method and use templates, the following provides the information you need to begin cutting pattern pieces for either the 7" or the 10 1/2" blocks.

Templates
• Cut 36:   A light (background rectangles)
• Cut 36:   B light (background squares)
• Cut 9:   B dark (center squares)
• Cut 36:   C dark (foot pads)
• Cut 144: D dark (toes—16 per block)
• Cut 144: D light (background 16—per block)

If you decide to use the speed technique, cut the following fabric strips (for a 7" block): from the light fabric(s), cut a strip(s) of fabric that is (are) 1 1/2" wide. If you are using 1/4 yard pieces, cut the strips the 9" direction and cut three strips per block. If you are using 1/2 yard pieces, cut the strips the 45" direction and cut three of each fabric. If you are using one-yard pieces, cut the

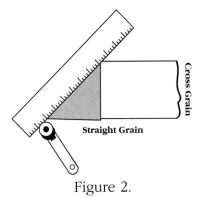

Figure 2.

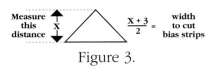

Measure this distance X $\dfrac{X+3}{2}$ = width to cut bias strips

Figure 3.

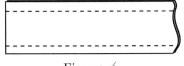

Figure 4.

Figure 5.

"Toe" Unit

Figure 6.

strips the 45" direction and cut five strips total. From these strips cut four 1 1/2" x 3 1/2" rectangles for each block (36 total). Also from these strips, cut four 1 1/2" squares for each block (36 total).

From the dark fabric(s), cut one strip 1 1/2" x 45" for the center squares. From that strip, cut one 1 1/2" square for each block (nine squares total). For the "foot pad," cut three strips 2 1/2" x 45". From these strips, cut four 2 1/2" squares for each block (36 total).

In making the "toes" for the Bear's Paw block, the bias strip-piecing technique will be used. Using the 1/4 yard, 1/2 yard or one-yard pieces of fabric, lay one dark piece of fabric right sides together with one light piece of fabric and raw edges even. Fold both layers of fabric down so that the straight grain will line up with the cross grain as shown in Figure 2. Using a straight edge and a rotary cutter, cut off the fold, leaving a true bias edge. Remove the triangle of fabric created.

Now determine how wide to cut the strips. The rule in bias strip piecing is to measure the height of the template to be used, including seam allowances. To this measurement, add 3" and divide by 2 (Figure 3). Then cut your fabric strips this width.

Keeping the light and dark strips right sides together, sew along *both* outer edges using a 1/4" seam (Figure 4).

Using a stiff template of pattern piece D (template plastic with sandpaper glued to the bottom works well), lay the template on the fabric so that the seamline on the template lines up with the sewn line on the bias strip. Carefully trace around the triangle. Continue marking triangles on both sides of the strip until you have the desired number of units (Figure 5).

Carefully cut on all marked lines. Open each unit to form a square (Figure 6) and finger press seam allowances toward the darker side.

Assemble the "feet" of the blocks as shown in Figure 7. Then, assemble each block as illustrated in Figure 8.

Feel free to play with different block arrangements. You

could put sashing between the blocks, set them on point, or alternate Bear's Paw blocks with solid blocks to create a larger quilt. Or try using an original setting!

It is a good idea to cut border strips after the quilt top is complete. If you have made your quilt blocks a different size or set blocks on point, the length of the borders must be adjusted. Check the size of your blocks, too. You might need to adjust border sizes if your blocks finish slightly larger or smaller than 7". Before adding the borders, make sure that your quilt is even. Fold it in half or measure it inside the seam allowances, rather than from outer edge to outer edge.

When you are ready to add the border to your quilt, press it to the quilt, right sides together and pin at regular intervals (approximately every 6"). This will help keep the edges of the quilt straight. Unless the border is to be mitered, sew the border strips to the quilt top in the following order: first to the top edge of the quilt, then to the bottom edge and finally, to each side of the quilt top.

The quilt, "Variable Bear's Paw," (#6A, page 31) has a 1/2" first border that was made from the same dark as the center 1 1/2" squares of each block (cut three strips 1" x 45"). After this border there is a 2" light-value border which is made of the tenth light fabric (cut three strips, 2 1/2" x 45"). The multiple borders in this quilt look like striped fabric, and the mitered corners enhance this effect. If you'd like to make a pieced border, there are many different ways to work with bias strip units. Some possibilities are shown in Figure 9.

Feel free to play with the pieced units and create other borders of your own. Corners might be a place to introduce creative design elements. When you have decided on a pieced border design, sew half-square triangle units together to form the pieced strips. Then attach your pieced border to the quilt as you did the other borders. Your original Bear's Paw quilt will be complete and ready for quilting!

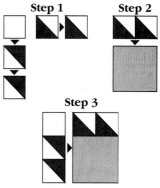

Figure 7.

Figure 8.

Figure 9.

What If...? Terrific Triangles

quilts shown on pages 34-36

❖ This design is primarily an exercise to get you working with fabric to create an original quilt. This can be a very freeing experience, but at the same time it might seem a bit scary. Cutting lots of triangles without knowing exactly how many red, how many white or how many blue you actually need might seem, at first, to be an impossible task.

For this quilt, pretend that you are an artist and that fabrics are your color palette. If an artist decides that he doesn't like one of the colors he has used in a painting he changes it. His concern is about the statement the painting will make when it is finished. In designing a quilt with triangles, you might have lots of them left over (perhaps the beginning of your next quilt). Or you might find that you have cut some triangles from a fabric you decide not to use at all. Does an artist feel that he must use up his entire tube of canary yellow before he can buy a different shade of yellow? Of course not—and neither should you. Remember, you are an artist, too, in the process of creating a masterpiece quilt!

The fabrics you select greatly affect the statements your quilts make. If you want a quilt to have an old or antique feel, choose fabrics typical of that kind of quilt, both in color and in type of print. I like to look for what I call "men's underwear" fabrics when I want to create an antique look. Colors typically used in antique quilts include turkey red, a mustardy shade of gold and Wedgwood blue. Browns and blacks will also help to "antique" a quilt. Remember that antique quilts were often made from true scraps left over from dresses and shirts.

If you are drawn to Amish-style quilts then you will gravitate naturally toward solid colors. The broader your palette, the more authentic your quilt will appear. And try incorporating several shades of black in your quilt, rather than just one. You might look through books of Amish quilts for color inspiration before you begin. There are two distinct palettes. The cool spectrum is typical of the Pennsylvania Amish—blues and greens, purples, fuchsias, blue grays, etc. Warm tones are often associated with the Indiana Amish—browns, olive greens, rusts, golds and yellow grays. Knowing which palette you prefer will be very helpful in selecting your solid colors.

You might choose to make an abstract, contemporary statement with your quilt. Color is one of the most important ingredients here. Closely related colors can yield a soft, subtle quilt, while high-contrast colors can produce a quilt almost jarring in its effect. Many abstract quilts use a lot of solid colors, although my quilt "A-Maze-ing" (#8F, page 36) uses only prints. Again, studying pictures of this style quilt, whether they are triangle quilts or not, can be helpful when you select fabrics for your contemporary quilt.

What about those of you who want to make a traditional, but not necessarily antique statement? For you, selecting fabric will be the simplest job of all. Keep in mind all of the principles of color value, contrast, and print scale that you would normally employ in making a quilt. If you're going to make a "snuggle" quilt for your daughter who adores blue and peach, look for fabrics in those tones. What you do with the triangles once they are cut will be a creative challenge in and of itself!

In general, fabrics should always be washed, and I prefer 100% cottons. New, unwashed fabrics contain sizing and additives which make them look crisp and smooth on the bolt, but these things might make it difficult for the fabrics to cling to your flannel wall.

I also believe that you can't have too many fabrics! I would start with no less than eight different fabrics—somewhere between eight and 80 would probably be sufficient! "Amish Terrific Triangles" (#8E, page 36) has almost 40 different solids.

Making sure that there is sufficient contrast between the light and dark values is also an important part of the design process. In the traditional/contemporary example, "Sharyn for the '80s" (#8C, page 35), I used only one light-value fabric but about 14 dark- and medium-value prints. (I won't tell you how many

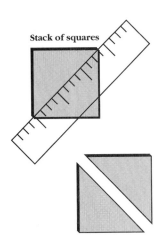

Figure 1.

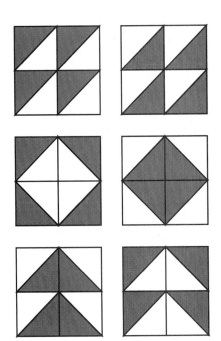

Figure 2.

fabrics I cut and *didn't* use!—I think of those as a *great* start on my next quilt!)

Cutting Triangles

Fold 44"/45"-wide fabric in half, selvage to selvage. Fold it in half again, bringing the fold to the selvages, and then make one more fold. This will give you a piece approximately 5" wide and eight thicknesses deep.

Lay your quilter's mini-rule (or strip template) across the fabric from fold to fold. Cut off the raw edges of your fabric with the rotary cutter and then slice through all eight layers to create a strip of fabric 4" wide. Then cut this strip into 4" squares. (Some people prefer to open the strip once and cut the squares through four layers. Depending on the actual width of your fabric, you might be able to cut a few extra squares this way.)

Lay the mini-rule from corner to corner of each stack of squares and cut them into equal half-square triangles. Repeat this process with each of your fabrics (Figure 1).

Creating the Design

I like to spread triangles out in stacks on an ironing board right beside my flannel wall. It's lots of fun to design quilts by putting up and taking down fabric triangles from this wall, and without it I doubt if my "Terrific Triangles #2" quilt (#8B, page 34) would ever have been created!

Remember, your quilt may look as random and unplanned or as controlled as you desire. This is *your* quilt, and *you* have to like it—don't be concerned about what someone else will think of it.

If you like the idea of proceeding with a trusting, free spirit, it can be fun to pick up the triangles and place them on the wall without any set pattern in mind. You could begin in the center and work outward in all directions, or begin in a corner and build consistently outward, picking up a color scheme that "feels" right for you. It is helpful, however, to know the direction you want the triangles to face, i.e. placement of light and dark values (Figure 2). If you decide you don't like what is happening, you can always switch things around. Relax, have fun, and let yourself go!

If a freewheeling approach doesn't seem to be going anywhere, or if that much freedom makes you feel a bit uneasy at first, try starting with what I call a "limited plan." For example, think of your triangle as half of a Log Cabin block. The traditional Log Cabin block is half dark and half light. If you put one light and one dark triangle together, then you are actually creating a pseudo-Log Cabin block. Any arrangement you can create with Log Cabin blocks can also be done with triangles. Why not try a Barn Raising set? Or Fields and Furrows? How about Light & Dark Variations, or a Zigzag set? (Figure 3)

Another type of limited plan is to begin with a traditional patchwork block which can be broken down into half-square triangles. Try laying out your triangles in that pattern. Your quilt could be a simple medallion, with one block centered and expanded by triangles that frame it. Your quilt blocks could also be repeated side by side or surrounded by sashing. What about a sampler? See Figure 4 for other possibilities for combining triangles in various configurations. They are illustrated in only light and dark values, so remember that the entire complexion of your quilt will change when different colors and varying values are introduced.

You don't have to stick to just triangle sets, either! If your design seems to be "calling out" for some squares or rectangles, and you don't want to sew like triangles together to create that image, then go ahead and cut a square or a rectangle or whatever else you might need for your quilt. *You* are the artist, and *you* set the rules.

During the design process, be sure to stand back from the wall frequently and analyze your quilt for color, line and design.

Barn Raising

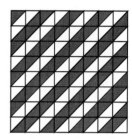
Fields and Furrows

Light & Dark Variation

Zigzag

Figure 3.

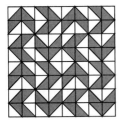

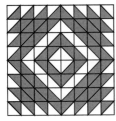

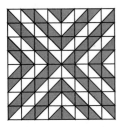

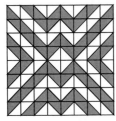

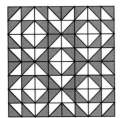

Figure 4.

If you're not happy with it, don't be afraid to start again! If several attempts still don't produce results you like, check your colors. Could there be one fabric which seems to "ruin" the others? Take it out! If your design seems "dull," consider introducing a new fabric—a "sparkler!" "A-Maze-ing" (#8F, page 36) has three red triangles in it. Without those three red units the quilt seemed flat. But more than three red triangles seemed to overpower the others and distracted my eye from the motion I was attempting to create. However, you can only put triangles up and down for so long before it is time to say, "Stop! This could go on *forever*—it's time to sew!"

Sewing

I wish there were a simple, efficient and speedy method of sewing this quilt but unfortunately, there isn't. Begin by sewing the triangles into squares, one pair at a time. It can be very easy to forget which side is dark and which side is light. I often say to myself out loud, "purple is on the left," as I lift the two triangles down, so that I can remember which way to put them back. You might like keeping a notebook beside your machine, too, in case of an interruption.

Once all of your triangles have been sewn into squares, you can begin stitching these squares together to form the quilt top. Begin at the top left and take down two squares. Stitch the vertical seam between this pair of squares, right sides together, as shown in Figure 5.

Without clipping the threads, pick up the two square units that were directly below the first two you worked with and stitch them together. Continue in this manner all the way down the left side of your quilt design, until you have stitched the bottom two squares together (Figure 6).

Take down each of the squares to the right of the pairs you have already joined and stitch them to the previously joined pairs of squares (Figure 7). Follow this process until you reach the last square at the bottom right side of the quilt top. At this point, you will have created several horizontal rows of squares (Figure 8). Now you can stitch the long seams between each row of squares, and your own unique "Terrific Triangles" quilt will be complete!

Borders

Your "Terrific Triangles" variation could be bordered like any other quilt, with plain border strips cut from the same (or similar) fabrics used in the quilt. A pieced border might also enhance the look of the quilt top. Try experimenting with 1 1/2" strips of fabric to create an unusual border. One possibility would be to sew 1 1/2" x 4" strips together lengthwise and create a border much like the one I used in my "Terrific Triangles #1" quilt (#8A, page 34). When I make this type of border I like to sew a plain border on the quilt before attaching the stripped border to avoid dealing with many seam allowances in such a small area. Corners can be handled by mitering or by inserting a plain square or two triangles sewn into a square unit (Figure 9).

Another possibility with stripped fabrics is to cut the segments so small that they become an accent border. This is an excellent way to draw color from the triangles in the body of the quilt, and the stripped border will almost appear to float when it is sandwiched between two plain borders. I used this type of border in "Amish Triangles" (#8E, page 36).

You might like to make a border from triangles—perhaps using them to "frame" the quilt, or using darker colored triangles to "stop" the eye at that part of the quilt. Think of the many triangle borders we have traditionally added to quilts—Flying Geese, Sawtooth, Dogtooth, Reverse Sawtooth. Draw from what is comfortable and personalize it to suit your own taste. Another use for fabric strips would be to piece them together and use them for binding your quilt—remember that this is *your* quilt.

Have lots of fun designing with Terrific Triangles!

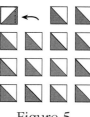

Figure 5.

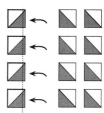

Figure 6.

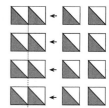

Figure 7.

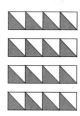

Figure 8.

Figure 9.

What If...? Pyramids Plus

quilts shown on pages 52-56

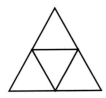

Figure 1.

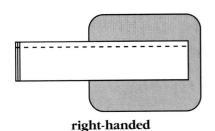

right-handed

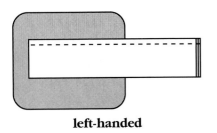

left-handed

Figure 2.

❖ This is a fantastic design and a great way to create a unique quilt. It is a good idea to experiment with this technique on a small quilt at first. The following suggestions will enable you to make a crib or lap-size quilt top approximately 25" x 40" without borders. You can expand on these ideas later to make larger quilts. You will need rotary cutting equipment, regular sewing equipment and a 30°/60°/90° plastic triangle (longest side at least 6 1/2" long).

The basic unit of this design is a four-triangle unit (Figure 1). Each two-strip combination you stitch will yield nine pairs of triangles, to which you will sew two loose triangles to complete the four-triangle unit. I like to work with a 3 1/2" x 45" strip width when I experiment with this design. There are several ways to combine these units, each resulting in a different look. Decide which of the following options you would like to use in your quilt and then you can determine how many strips of fabric to cut.

• Option #1:

8 dark strips and 8 light strips. Each dark strip should be a different dark print, each light strip a different light print. Make sure that the dark strips are really dark and that they are all close in value. The light prints should also be close in value. You could use totally different light and dark *colors*, as long as you have good contrast between the lights and darks.

• Option #2:

8 strips of color #1 and 8 strips of color #2. This option requires only two colors; for example, red as color #1 and black as color #2. You will use 8 different red prints and 8 different black prints, again making sure that the fabrics of each color are similar in value. Varying the scale of each print is also a good idea. Another possibility is to create a monochromatic quilt by using contrasting values of the same color, i.e. light blues and dark blues.

• Option #3:

6 strips each of colors #1, #2 and #3. Again, the secret is to use

similar values within each color, but to have a lot of contrast between colors. This option can be as simple as using three colors; black (dark), gray (medium) and white (light). Or choose any three colors you like as long as they are contrasting. This option requires a bit more fabric, but the results can be spectacular!

It is also possible to design a quilt with pieced pyramid units and solid pyramids. For a solid pyramid, cut a strip of fabric exactly as wide as the height of the pieced pyramid unit. Cut the solid pyramids in the same way as the pieced pyramid units are cut. This is one way of making a larger quilt with less piecing involved. If you decide you want to add some solid pyramids, you can get nine solid pyramids from approximately 1/4 yard of fabric.

When you have chosen the option you prefer, you can begin to cut fabric. You will need a total of either 16 or 18 strips of fabric. The strips could be cut any width, as long as the width is the same for all of the strips. You will always need an even number of strips in the same color family or value.

To begin sewing, set the stitch length on your machine to 12 stitches per inch. Place two strips of different fabrics (same value or color) right sides together, and seam them together along one long edge with a 1/4" seam allowance. Continue sewing all your strips together in this manner. Layer the strips one on top of another, three pairs deep (six layers of fabric). Match the long seamed edges and the short edges at one end of the stacked strips, leaving the uneven edges together at the opposite end. Right-handed people should place the even edges of the strips at the right-hand edge of the mat. Left-handed people should place the even edges of the strips at the left-hand edge of the mat (Figure 2).

Position your plastic triangle as illustrated in Figure 3. Right-handed people cut along the right edge of the triangle. Left-handed people cut along the left edge. Flip the triangle over, matching the 60° angle exactly at the top edge of the strip where the last cut ended. Make sure the short side of the triangle matches the cut edges of the strips (Figure 4).

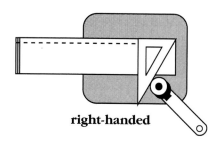

right-handed

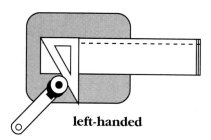

left-handed

Figure 3.

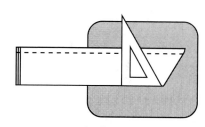

right-handed

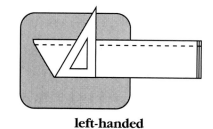

left-handed

Figure 4.

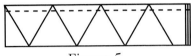
Figure 5.

Figure 6.

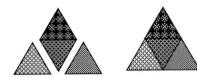
Figure 7.

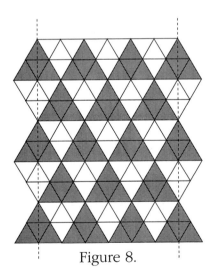
Figure 8.

Continue along the entire strip in this manner, and repeat this process with the rest of your strips (Figure 5).

Now separate the cut pieces into like units (Figure 6). There will be some units with stitching through the points—remove these stitches. These two loose triangles will be used in making the four-triangle unit. Open each two-triangle unit and carefully finger press toward the darker fabric. At this point, you can complete the four-triangle unit by attaching two loose triangles of contrasting fabrics (Figure 7).

Do not trim triangle extensions or worry about grainline on units. You will be dealing with bias edges on every piece. After you have constructed your four-triangle pyramids, press each unit carefully. This will help them stick to the flannel wall. You can now begin to design your own Pyramids Plus quilt.

Once you have decided on the overall design, you're ready to sew the units together into rows. Match the triangle tip extensions on the four-triangle units as you stitch them together. (It's just like matching notches when sewing a garment!) Looking for straight rows will help avoid set-in piecing. I like to stitch the quilt top in the following sequence:

• Sew the units together in straight rows across, beginning in the upper left corner.
• Finger press the seam allowances toward the triangles on the right.
• Stitch two rows together and press carefully. Be sure to avoid pressing the outer (bias) edges as much as possible.
• To form the quilt top, sew the rows together and press.
• Press the quilt top carefully (all of the outer edges will be bias).
• In order to straighten the sides of your quilt, cut through the partial units on each side after the top is finished. Be sure to trim 1/4" beyond the last finished four-triangle unit (Figure 8).

Have fun making your own unique quilt—what you see on these pages is only the tip of the pyramid!

❖ This quilt can be as "scrappy" or as color controlled as you like. In "Too Many Ties" (#3A, page 25), I used one light and 45 different dark prints. You could make the entire quilt in only two fabrics, one light and one dark. Or you can use any number of light and dark fabrics you wish.

If you are purchasing fabric for this quilt, multiply the number of strips of a given fabric needed by 3" and then add an extra 1/8 yard to allow for folding as directed in the strip-cutting instructions on pages 64-65. Out of 1/4 yard of fabric you could probably get two strips. However, when purchasing fabric it is good to allow for shrinkage and distortion that could occur when you prewash.

The original Bow Tie block was designed with set-in pieces surrounding the "tie." I have added lines which greatly simplify the piecing process. What used to be a difficult block is now a snap, both to cut and to piece. And the final results "read" the same (Figure 1).

The basic Bow Tie block is based on a four-patch grid; i.e. for a finished 5" block, each division of the block would be equal to 1 1/4" (Figure 2). If you want your block to be a different size you can assign a different measurement to each block division. For example, 1/2" divisions result in a 2" block, 1" divisions will form a 4" block, and a 2" division creates an 8" block. (Full-size pattern pieces for 4", 5", 6" and 8" finished blocks are given on page 91.)

Refer to the chart below to determine how many fabric strips to cut for the background pieces in your quilt.*

What If...? Ties 'R Us

quilts shown on pages 24-26

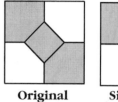

| Original Bow Tie | Simplified Bow Tie |

Figure 1.

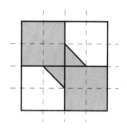

four 1 1/4" divisions = 5" block

Figure 2.

Fabric Requirements			
Size	Rows	Blocks	3" strips**
crib: 40" x 40"	8 x 8	64	16 dark, 11 light
nap: 40" x 60"	8 x 12	96	24 dark, 16 light
twin: 40" x 75"	8 x 15	120	30 dark, 16 light
full/queen: 60" x 90"	12 x 18	216	54 dark, 36 light
king: 80" x 90"	16 x 18	298	72 dark, 48 light

*All sizes are based on 5" finished blocks. No allowance has been made for borders.
**Each 3" strip of dark will yield 4 Bow Tie blocks. Each 3" strip of light will yield 6 blocks.

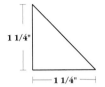

Figure 3.

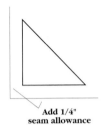

Add 1/4"
seam allowance

Figure 4.

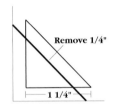

Remove 1/4"

1 1/4"

Figure 5.

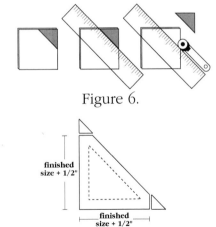

Figure 6.

finished
size + 1/2"

finished
size + 1/2"

Figure 7.

Leaving the strips folded in fourths, eliminate the selvage/fold edges. Next, cut three 3" squares through all four layers of fabric. This yields a total of twelve 3" squares. You will need two 3" squares for each block you make, so you can construct backgrounds for six blocks from one strip of background fabric.

When I cut the pieces for the ties, I like to use a Speedy. This technique for cutting triangles that are to be sewn to oddly shaped pieces was developed by Trudie Hughes. (Refer to page 81 for information about Trudies Hughes' *Template Free Quiltmaking* book series.*) One section of the Bow Tie block consists of squares with the corners cut off and triangles sewn back on. By using a Speedy you can cut off the correct amount of fabric from the squares, cut the proper size triangles and they will fit together accurately.

A Speedy looks like a template, but it is used differently. To draft your Speedy, begin by drawing (on graph paper) the finished triangle size that will be sewn back onto the corners. In this case (for a 5" block), that will be 1 1/4" along the shorter edges (Figure 3). After you have drawn this triangle, add a 1/4" seam allowance along both short edges (Figure 4). Then remove 1/4" from the diagonal edge (Figure 5).

Trace onto stiff template plastic to make a Speedy. Then stack squares of fabric in at least four layers and position the Speedy in one corner. Place the mini-ruler securely against it. This positions the ruler exactly at the place you will cut. Move the Speedy aside and use your rotary cutter right next to the ruler to cut through all of the layers of fabric (Figure 6). The fabric triangle to be sewn back onto that edge will be the same size triangle you used to make the Speedy, but now it must have a 1/4" seam allowance added to all three sides.

Trimming the tips of these triangles will help you fit them precisely onto the squares. Take a stack of triangles and measure the finished size of the triangle plus 1/2" along both short edges. Cut the edges off as illustrated in Figure 7.

Now you are ready to construct the Bow Tie blocks. Position the dark triangles to the light shapes, right sides together as shown in Figure 8.

Chain sew the units, lifting the presser foot between units. This will allow space between the units with minimal waste of thread (Figure 9). Clip the units apart and finger press the seam allowances toward the dark triangles.

Lay out the blocks and stack units on top of each other so that you have all of the blocks in one stack (Figure 10). Take the top two units of the first block and stitch, right sides together (Figure 11). Chain sew the remaining units until all units have been stitched (Figure 12). Clip threads after every two units (each pair of units forms one block).

Open the block units and finger press the seam allowances toward the dark squares. Then fold the block units together horizontally, making sure that the seam allowances alternate, and sew the center seam (Figure 13). Chain sew all of the blocks together in this way, clip them apart and press carefully.

You are now ready to design your quilt. Because the Bow Tie is a directional block, there is much you can do with this design. Don't be afraid to try something really different. What if you set the blocks on point? Or what if you used sashings between the blocks? How about using an alternating set? Try placing the blocks in different directions—new configurations can create wonderful designs. Have fun—you'll probably end up finding so many different arrangements you like, you'll want to make more than one quilt!

---

*Trudie Hughes' 3-book series, *Template-Free Quiltmaking*, is available through That Patchwork Place, Inc., PO Box 118, Bothell, WA 98041. Trudie has also designed two rulers, the Rotary Rule™ and the Rotary Mate™, to be used with the rotary cutter for template-free quiltmaking. For more information, write to Patched Works, 13330 Watertown Plank Road, Elm Grove, WI 53122.

Figure 8.

Figure 9.

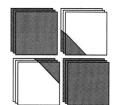

Figure 10.

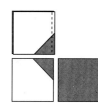

Figure 11.

Figure 12.

Alternate seam allowances

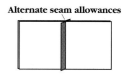

Figure 13.

What If...? Attic Windows

quilts shown on pages 50-51

❖ There is so much you can do with the Attic Windows concept that I hesitate to set any guidelines about color selection or yardage. Yet I also realize that we all need a place to begin. For that reason I will make a few suggestions, but please don't let them stop you from experimenting!

The following yardage and strip-cutting charts are based on using one fabric throughout the quilt for the "pane" (the inside section). It is also assumed that the panes will be square, but neither assumption has to be absolute. The panes could be cut from more than one fabric, and the block could be rectangular (or even triangular)! For that matter, the panes don't even have to be the same size throughout your quilt!

Yardage And Strip-Cutting Chart
4 1/2" finished block (3" pane)

	Crib	Twin	Double/Queen
• Size:	36" x 40 1/2"	72" x 85 1/2"	85 1/2 x 94 1/2"
• Set:	8 x 9	16 x 19	19 x 21
• # of Blocks:	72	304	399
	Yardage	**Yardage**	**Yardage**
• Panes:	21" = 3/4 yd.	91" = 2 3/4 yd.	117" = 3 1/2 yd.
• Sills:	16" = 5/8 yd.	68" = 1 1/8 yd.	90" = 2 3/4 yd.
• Sashes:	16" = 5/8 yd.	68" = 1 1/8 yd.	90" = 2 3/4 yd.
	Strips to Cut	**Strips to Cut**	**Strips to Cut**
• Panes:	6 at 3 1/2"	26 at 3 1/2"	34 at 3 1/2"
• Sills:	8 at 2"	34 at 2"	45 at 2"
• Sashes:	8 at 2"	34 at 2"	45 at 2"

PER STRIP YIELD
• Panes: 42" divided by 3 1/2" = 12 per strip
• Sashes and sills: The above numbers assume that all sashes and or sills are cut in the same direction. To do this, the strip must be opened up and the pieces cut one at a time. The yield then is 9 per strip, cut in one direction: ▰ . Double folding the strip to give you rights and lefts of each fabric will yield 8 per strip, 4 of each image, as shown: ▰ ▰ .
Yardage and strip requirements for double-cut sashes and sills:
   • Crib: 9 strips at 2" = 18" (5/8 yd) • Twin: 38 strips at 2" = 76" (1 3/8 yd)
   • Double/Queen: 50 strips at 2" = 100" (3 yds)

Yardage And Strip-Cutting Chart
6" finished block (4 1/2" pane)

	Crib	Twin	Double/Queen
• Size:	36" x 42"	72" x 84"	84" x 96"
• Set:	6 x 7	12 x 14	14 x 16
• # of Blocks:	42	168	224
	Yardage	**Yardage**	**Yardage**
• Panes:	30" = 1 yd.	105" = 3 1/8 yd.	140" = 4 1/8 yd.
• Sills:	12" = 1/2 yd.	48" = 1 1/2 yd.	64" = 2 yd.
• Sashes:	12" = 1/2 yd.	48" = 1 1/2 yd.	64" = 2 yd.
	Strips to Cut	**Strips to Cut**	**Strips to Cut**
• Panes:	6 at 5"	21 at 5"	28 at 5"
• Sills:	6 at 2"	24 at 2"	32 at 2"
• Sashes:	6 at 2"	24 at 2"	32 at 2"

PER STRIP YIELD
• Panes: 42" divided by 5" = 8 per strip
• Sashes and sills: The above numbers assume all sashes and/or sills are cut in the same direction. The strip must be opened up and the pieces cut one at a time. The yield is 7 per strip.

If you wish to double cut the sashes and sills with the strips folded to give you rights and lefts of each fabric, then the yield is reduced to 6 per strip. The yardage and strip requirements would be as follows for the double-cut sashes and sills:

• Crib: 7 strips at 2" = 14" (5/8 yd) • Twin: 28 strips at 2" = 56" (1 3/4 yd)
• Double/Queen: 38 strips at 2" = 76" (2 3/8 yd)

Quilt sizes given are for blocks only, and do not include borders. Take this into consideration when selecting quilt size and purchasing fabric if you wish to make a quilt with borders. If you'll be making a scrappy attic windows quilt, refer to the strip chart and cut the total number of strips from a variety of fabrics.

There are many other things you can do with the panes, besides using one fabric. What if you placed a pieced block, such as a simple star, in the pane position? Or an appliquéd block? How about photo-transfer prints of family members? Embellishments like these can give you many creative options.

The information in the charts also refers to three-fabric quilts that have one particular fabric in each of the three positions—pane, sill and sash. However, it can be great fun to play with

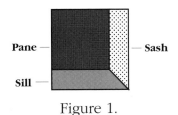

Figure 1.

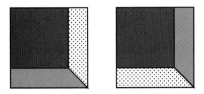

Figure 2.

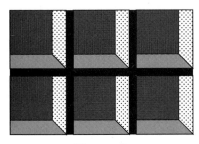

Figure 3.

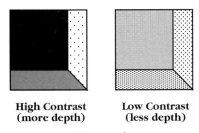

High Contrast   **Low Contrast**
(more depth)   **(less depth)**

Figure 4.

scraps, as well. In many Attic Window quilts, we see the sashes and sills made of scraps while the pane fabric remains constant.

In the "traditional" Attic Window quilt, the color values are also held constant for each of the three parts of the window (Figure 1).

The chart assumes that color values are consistent throughout the quilt. But what if you made some windows with medium value for the sill, and some with medium value for the sashes (Figure 2)?

Another fun experiment is the addition of lattice strips between each of the windows, which creates more depth of field (Figure 3). Lattice strips can be added in exactly the same way that you would add them to any traditional quilt. If you decide you might like the look of an additional lattice strip, keep in mind that it should contrast with the three fabrics used in the window.

The illusion of depth can be created through the use of different prints, but also through value change. The higher the contrast in value between the three parts of the window, the farther away the background feels, thus creating more depth. The closer the values of the three parts are to one another, the flatter the field becomes and the closer the background appears to be (Figure 4).

A small, busy print in the pane section will make the background appear farther away. A large-scale print will make the background appear closer (Figure 5). You can use a printed panel as a story-like scene in the pane, but it is tricky to place the image exactly the same way in each window. It is easy to lose part of the image due to space taken up by the sills and sashes.

Cutting

Begin with the panes. Consult the yardage charts for fabric requirements and the correct number of strips to cut. The charts are based on using square panes. Leave each fabric strip folded in fourths and lay it on the mat so that the selvage/fold edge is together (on the left for right-handed people, and on the right for left-handers). Remove the selvage/fold edge and cut the four layers into squares that are equal to the width of the fabric strip. For example, 3 1/2" strips yield 3 1/2" squares (the panes will be 3" finished) and 5" strips yield 5" squares (the panes will be 4 1/2" finished). You will need one pane for each attic window block. Refer to "# of blocks" on the chart to see how many you will need.

Next, cut the sills and sashes. Cutting them facing the correct direction is the key consideration here (the sashes point one direction, and sills, the other). To achieve this, start with the strips for your sashes. Open the fabric strips up completely. Layer four strips on top of one another, each right side up. Position the sash template *right side up* on the strip, and carefully cut sashes down the entire length of the strip (Figure 6). You will need one sash for each block.

Now unfold your fabric strips for the sills, again placing four strips on top of one another, right side up. This time, place the template *wrong side up*, and carefully cut sills down the entire length of the strip (Figure 7). You will also need one sill for each block.

Sewing Sequence

Begin with the pane piece underneath and the sashing piece on top, right sides together, as illustrated in Figure 8. Sew the entire length of the seam. You may chain stitch additional units, one after another, without clipping threads, until all of the sash/pane units have been sewn. Then open up the units and finger press the seam allowances carefully toward the sash pieces, as shown in Figure 9.

Layer these pane/sash units one on top of another, wrong side up, with the sash piece at the bottom. Now you are ready to sew the sills to the pane/sash units. Position the sill piece underneath the pane/sash unit, right sides together, as shown in

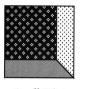

Small Print   **Large Print**
(appears further away)   **(appears closer)**

Figure 5.

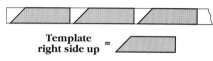

Template right side up =

Figure 6.

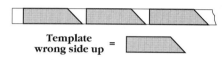

Template wrong side up =

Figure 7.

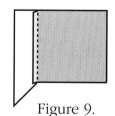

Figure 8.

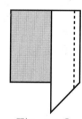

Figure 9.

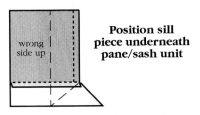

Position sill piece underneath pane/sash unit

Figure 10.

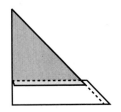

Figure 11.

Figure 10. Beginning at the outer edge, stitch up to the previous sewing line. You must lock the stitches at this point, either by backstitching or stitching in place two or three times. Continue chain piecing these units through the machine. It isn't necessary to stop and cut the thread each time, but you will need to move each finished unit back from your machine a bit before starting the next seam. Do cut excess threads away before going on to the next step, however.

To miter the corner of the block, hold the sash and sill so that the diagonal edges match up (Figure 11). Insert the machine needle at the start of the previous stitching line and drop the pressure foot. Lock your stitching at this point, then continue sewing all the way to the outer edge. Repeat this step with each unit.

Finger press seam allowances away from the pane. The mitered corner can be either directionally pressed, or pressed open if you feel that the units will lie better. Use the iron at this time, if you like.

Once you have constructed all the blocks you need, play with setting them on point. We are used to seeing them set straight because that's the way real windows are oriented, but they don't have to represent windows!

Take your blocks to the flannel wall. Think of them as the asymmetrical blocks they are. Turn and tilt them to see what patterns you can create. There is no telling how many fun variations you can find!

Once you've decided on an overall design, you can proceed to sew the blocks together. Add borders, if you wish. Your original attic windows design is now ready for quilting.

❖ When I saw Elizabeth Croy's delightful scrap quilt, "Confetti," in *Traditional Quiltworks #7*, my mind began spinning with the many creative possibilities this quilt design offered. I like to use strip piecing whenever possible, and I immediately began to convert this design to strip-piecing methods.

The biggest decision I faced was how to color the block. The coloration possibilities for this block are endless. When you have decided on the coloration you like, you can determine the number and color of the strips you need. I am providing two examples for color possibilities here, along with their respective strip rows and yardage requirements. Following these examples and substituting your own color combinations will enable you to create an original Confetti quilt variation.

For the first example (see pages 60-61), I used 11 hand-dyed shades of one color for the "chain," and one black for the entire background. The colors in the chain are numbered diagonally in the diagram, from lightest to darkest, beginning at the lower left corner. I have designated the background as "B" wherever it occurs in the block. I assigned the measurement of 1 1/4" to each row, which results in a finished 7 1/2" block. (Remember, if a strip row *finishes* at 1 1/4", it must be *cut* at 1 3/4".) It takes six rows to create this block and they are numbered in order, as shown in Figure 1.

The background fabric must be cut into strips of varying widths, to complete each strip row as shown in Figure 2. Following the cutting instructions, cut each strip (from selvage to selvage) in the following widths.

Cutting
Of background fabric, cut:
- 2 strips at 5 1/2"
- 2 strips at 4 1/4"
- 2 strips at 3"
- 2 strips at 1 3/4"

What If... Confetti Quilt

quilts shown on page 49

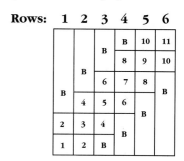

Figure 1.

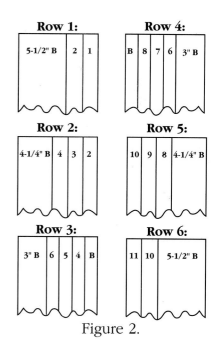

Figure 2.

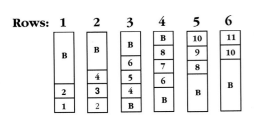

Figure 3.

Of the chain fabrics, cut:
- 1 strip at 1 3/4" of each odd-numbered fabric (see Figure 1)
- 2 strips at 1 3/4" of each even-numbered fabric (see Figure 1)

When you have all of the strips cut, assemble them into the strip row combinations indicated in Figure 2.

Cut these sewn rows into 1 3/4" segments, as illustrated in Figure 3.

Sew these segmented rows together to form the block, using 1/4" seam allowances and pressing seams toward the darker fabric. Now you're ready to put these blocks on your flannel wall and start designing your quilt.

For my second example of the Confetti block (#17B, page 49), I used only three fabrics: one background fabric and two complementary colors for the chains. It takes two different blocks to create this look (Figure 4).

It takes only three strip rows to make either block, since in *both* Block A and Block B, row 1 is the same as row 6, row 2 is the same as row 5 and row 3 is the same as row 4.

For a quilt that has twelve blocks, cut the following total number of strips:

Of background fabric:
- 6 strips at 1 3/4"
- 2 strips at 5 1/2"
- 2 strips at 4 1/2"
- 2 strips at 3"

Of the chain fabrics:
- 6 strips (fabric #1) at 1 3/4"
- 6 strips (fabric #2) at 1 3/4"

Sew the strips together to form strip rows for Block A and Block B as illustrated in Figure 5.

Rows:

1	2	3	4	5	6
			B	2	1
		B	2	B	2
	B		2	B	2
B		2	B	2	B
	2	B	2	B	
2	B	2		B	
1	2	B			

Block A

Rows:

1	2	3	4	5	6
			B	1	2
		B	1	B	1
	B		1	B	1
B		1	B	1	B
	1	B	1	B	
1	B	1		B	
2	1	B			

Block B

Figure 4.

Segment these sewn rows into 1 3/4" sections. Stitch the rows together to form Blocks A and B, using a 1/4" seam allowance and pressing seams toward the darker fabric (Figure 6).

When the blocks are complete, it's time to have fun playing on your flannel wall with different combinations. Any of the arrangements you can make with the first block variation can also be made by using these blocks. There are so many possible configurations, you may want to make several quilts!

Here are some more ideas for you to consider: what if you were to shade the chain fabrics from lightest to darkest, as I did in my first example, but without regard to color? In other words, any *colors* could be used, as long as they were placed in positions from lightest to darkest *value*. What would this type of quilt look like?

What if you applied the color theory of overlapping (or transparency) to the chain itself? What happens when blue and yellow overlap? You get green. By placing one blue and one yellow on either side of the chain, with a green in the center position, it would look as though the yellow and blue fabrics overlapped and produced green! Starting to get the idea?

What if you shaded the chain from light to dark and *back* to light again?

When you start playing on a flannel wall, it might help to think of the Confetti block as a cousin of the Log Cabin block. Utilize the directional look of the Log Cabin block to create visual movement in your Confetti quilt. Try a Barn Raising, Fields and Furrows, or Zigzag set! And keep in mind, as always, that *you* are the artist creating this quilt. Play on the flannel wall with as many different designs as you can dream up—and enjoy yourself!

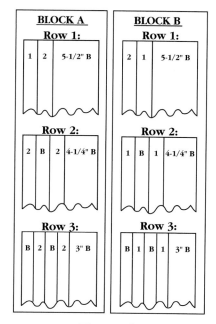

Figure 5.

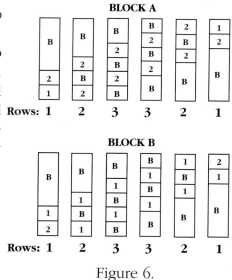

Figure 6.

89

Full-Size Pattern Pieces

7" Bears Paw Pattern Pieces

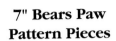

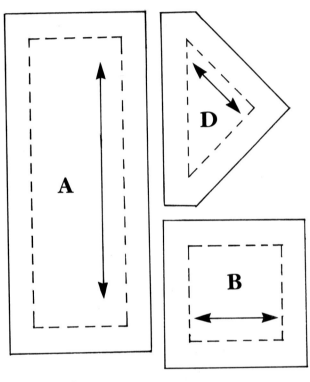

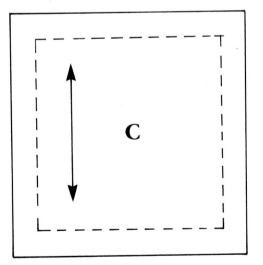

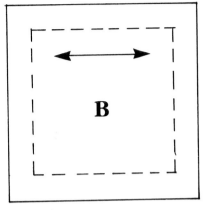

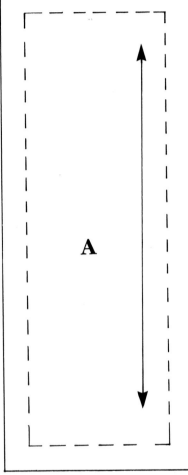

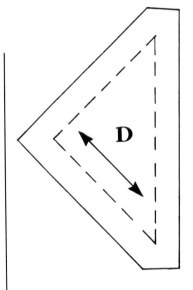

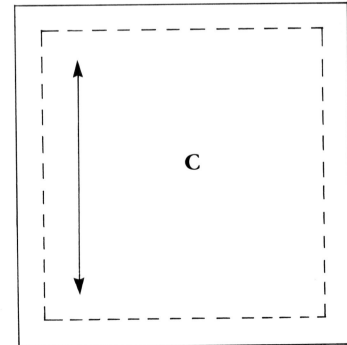

90

Attic Windows
Pattern Pieces

Use the desired sill/sash pattern for your attic windows blocks.

To make template, start at baseline and trace to desired size.

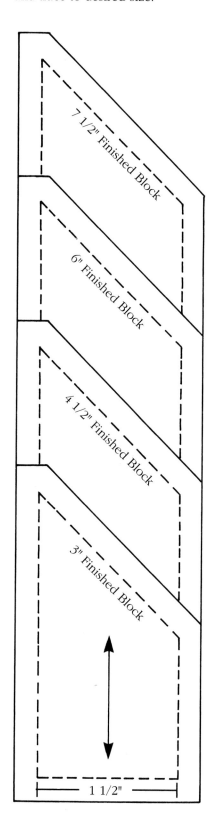

7 1/2" Finished Block

6" Finished Block

4 1/2" Finished Block

3" Finished Block

1 1/2"

Ties 'R Us
Pattern Pieces

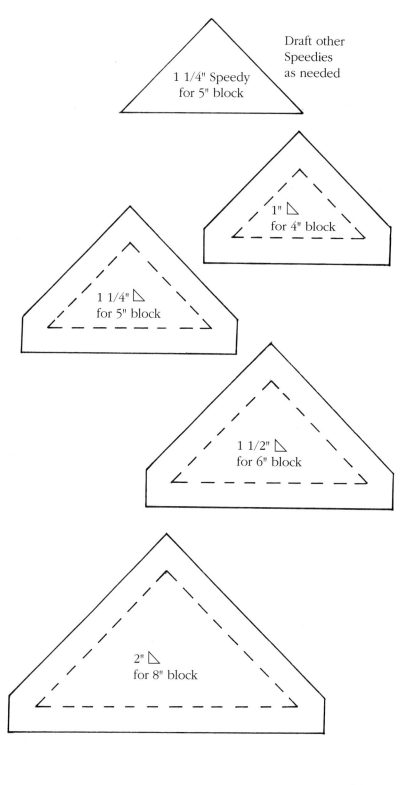

1 1/4" Speedy
for 5" block

Draft other Speedies as needed

1"
for 4" block

1 1/4"
for 5" block

1 1/2"
for 6" block

2"
for 8" block

WORKSHEET

1. Source for inspiration _____
             (book, magazine, page, location, etc.)

2. Anticipated Changes: (color, scale, block, set, size, orientation)

        1)   4)

        2)   5)

        3)   6)

3. To be "retained" from the original _____

_____

4. "Recipe" or "Formula" for quilt:

   1) Block to be used _____

   2) Scale (size of block) _____

   3) Templates needed _____

   4) Fabric Determination: Scrap? Control? Number of Fabrics to be used? _____

_____

   5) Anticipated number of blocks to make _____

   6) Anticipated finished size quilt to make _____

   7) "Look" or "Feel" desired from finished project _____

_____

5. My personal goal from this experience and this quilt is _____

_____

_____

Quilt Credits

❖ Sharyn Squire Craig made all of the quilts except the following (quilts listed by #): Renee Charity, 2C; Linda Packer, 3C, 3D; Debbie McCarter, 5B; Cheryl Morris, 6C; Linda Sawry, 6D; Sandi Justice, 6E; Sharon Kostink, 6F; Ettie Ellen Brees, 7; Jean Tebo, 7B; Eunice Farrer Chamberlain, 9; Emily Packer, 9A, 20A; Anne Bashore Stouffer, 11; Margaret Steele Entrekin, 12; Linda Hamby, 12A; Marsha McCloskey, 13; Charlotte Ballard, 14; Ione Skaar, 14A; Susan Deborah Timby, 15; Alvia Troutt, 16; Donna Baker, 16B; Sandy Anderson, 16C, 19C; Becky Zorn, 16D; Louise Hixon, 16E; Kris Zook, 16F; Elizabeth Croy, 17; Linda Packer, 17A; Judy Florence, 18; Laurine Leeke, 18C, 19E, 19F; Carol O'Brien, 18B; and Patty Barney, 19G. The quiltmakers of 2, 3, 4, 5, 6, 9, 10, 11B and 19 are unknown.

Photo Credits

❖ All quilts were photographed by Ken Jacques except the following: Steve Appel, 3, 13, 16, 17; Susan Einstein, 4; Myron Miller, 5; Sharon Risedorph and Lynn Kellner, 8; Terry Wild, 11B, 12; Brent Kane, 14; Jim Christofferson, 18; and Metro Photographics, picture on back cover. Photographs courtesy of: Jonathan Holstein, 2, 19; American Quilters' Society, 7, 7B; Roderick Kiracofe, 9; Cyril Nelson and E.P. Dutton, 10, 11; Gail Binney-Stiles, 20.

Special Thanks

❖ I offer special thanks to the following for permitting me to publish a quilt from their collection: Christiane Meunier, publisher, Chitra Publications; Gail Binney-Stiles, author and quiltmaker; Roger Tebo, husband of the late quiltmaker Jean Tebo; and Marsha McCloskey, author and quiltmaker. I am also grateful to the following for permission to publish and/or for supplying their color transparencies: Jonathan Holstein, quilt historian; Wilma Mattioli and Jeanette Lasansky of Pennsylvania's Oral Traditions Project; Nancy Martin and Marion Shelton, publisher and editorial assistant, That Patchwork Place; Rita Barber; Roderick Kiracofe, publisher, RK Press; Myron Miller; Lady's Circle Patchwork Quilts; Cyril Nelson, editor, E. P. Dutton; Carter Houck; Bill and Meredith Schroeder, publishers, American Quilters' Society; Lynda Milligan; Nancy Smith; Orlan and Fay Swennes, owners of Cabin Fever Calicoes; and Chilton Book Company. I am also greatly indebted to all the quiltmakers whose creations are the heart of this book.

Suggested Reading

Barber, Rita. *Quilts and Quilters from Illinois*. Paducah, KY: American Quilters' Society, 1986.

Binney, Edwin 3rd and Gail Binney-Winslow. *Homage to Amanda*. San Francisco: RK Press, 1984.

Florence, Judy. *A Collection of Favorite Quilts*. Paducah, KY: American Quilter's Society, 1990.

Florence, Judy. *Award Winning Scrap Quilts*. Greensboro, NC: Wallace-Homestead Book Co., 1987.

Holstein, Jonathan. *Pieced Quilt: an American Design Tradition*. Boston: Little Brown & Co., 1973.

Horton, Roberta. *Calico and Beyond*. Martinez, CA: C&T Publishing, 1987.

Houck, Carter and Cyril Nelson. *Treasury of American Quilts*. New York: E.P. Dutton, 1982.

Hughes, Trudie. *Template-Free Quiltmaking*. Bothell, WA: That Patchwork Place, 1986.

Kile, Michael and Roderick Kiracofe (ed.). *Quilt Digest #2*. San Francisco: Quilt Digest Press, 1984.

Knox, Gerald. (ed.) *Better Homes and Gardens American Patchwork & Quilting*. Des Moines: Meredith Corp., 1985.

Lasansky, Jeanette. *Pieced by Mother*. Lewisburg, PA: Pennsylvania Oral Traditions Project, 1987.

Leone, Diana. *Attic Windows: A Contemporary View*. Los Altos, CA: Leone Publications, 1988.

Marston, Gwen and Joe Cunningham. *Sets and Borders*. Paducah, KY: American Quilters' Society, 1987.

Martin, Judy. *Patchworkbook*. New York: Chas. Scribner's Sons, 1983.

Martin, Judy. *Scraps, Blocks & Quilts*. Denver: Crosley-Griffith Publishing Co., 1990.

Martin, Judy. *Ultimate Book of Quilt Block Patterns*. Denver: Crosley-Griffith Publishing Co., 1988.

Martin, Nancy. *A Banner Year*. Bothell, WA: That Patchwork Place, 1989.

McCloskey, Marsha. *Feathered Star Quilts*. Bothell, WA: That Patchwork Place, 1987.

McClun, Diana and Laura Nownes. *Quilts Galore*. San Francisco: Quilt Digest Press, 1990.

McClun, Diana and Laura Nownes. *Quilts! Quilts! Quilts! The Complete Guide to Quiltmaking*. San Francisco: Quilt Digest Press, 1988.

Mulligan, Lynda and Nancy Smith. *Pineapple Passion*. Bothell, WA: That Patchwork Place, 1989.

Nephew, Sara. *Building Block Quilts*. Bothell, WA: That Patchwork Place, 1990.

Nephew, Sara. *Quilts from a Different Angle*. Bothell, WA: That Patchwork Place, 1987.

Pottinger, David. *Quilts from the Indiana Amish*. New York: E.P. Dutton, 1983.

Quilt Engagement Calendar. New York: E.P. Dutton (any year).

Shirer, Marie. *Quilt Settings*. Wheatridge, CO: Moon Over the Mountain, 1989.

Singer Quilting by Machine. Editors of the Singer Sewing Reference Library. Minnetonka, MN: Cy Decosse, Inc., 1990.

Traditional Quiltworks magazine. New Milford, PA: Chitra Publications. October 1988-.

Walker, Michele. *The Complete Book of Quiltmaking*. New York: Alfred A. Knopf, 1986.